RELATING TO ADOLESCENTS

Educators in a Teenage World

Susan Eva Porter

Rowman & Littlefield Education
Lanham • New York • Toronto • Plymouth, UK

Published in the United States of America
by Rowman & Littlefield Education
A Division of Rowman & Littlefield Publishers, Inc.
A wholly owned subsidiary of The Rowman & Littlefield Publishing Group, Inc.
4501 Forbes Boulevard, Suite 200, Lanham, Maryland 20706
www.rowmaneducation.com

Estover Road
Plymouth PL6 7PY
United Kingdom

This book was placed by the Educational Design Services LLC Literary Agency.

British Library Cataloguing in Publication Information Available

Library of Congress Cataloging-in-Publication Data

Porter, Susan Eva, 1963–
  Relating to adolescents: educators in a teenage world / Susan Eva Porter.
    p. cm.
  Includes bibliographical references.
  ISBN 978-1-60709-058-8 (cloth: alk. paper)
  ISBN 978-1-60709-059-5 (pbk.: alk. paper)
  ISBN 978-1-60709-060-1 (e-book)
  1. High school teaching—United States. 2. Middle school teaching—
United States. 3. Teenagers—Education—United States. 4. Teacher-student
relationships—United States. 5. Teenagers and adults—United States.
I. Title.
  LB1737.U6P67 2009
  373.1102—dc22

                                                    2008049251

∞ ™ The paper used in this publication meets the minimum requirements of
American National Standard for Information Sciences—Permanence of Paper
for Printed Library Materials, ANSI/NISO Z39.48-1992.
Manufactured in the United States of America.

To Mum,
the first teacher I ever knew.
I hope you're watching,
wherever you are.

CONTENTS

ACKNOWLEDGMENTS

I have known and befriended many teachers throughout my career. I could not have written this book without their inspiration and support.

A few special educators and clinicians helped me stay focused along the way, and to them I owe many thanks. Nell Branco, Travis Brownley, Liz Katz, Sande Kiriluk, Rachel Stettler, Peter Thorp, and Jessica Tighe served as wise and gentle readers. I want to extend special thanks to my former professor, Ted Sizer, for giving this work his time and attention, and for his very generous feedback. And to Michael Brosnan, of *Independent School* magazine, whose careful reading and comments kept me buoyed.

My beautiful sisters didn't do much for me throughout this process, but they'd kill me if I didn't acknowledge them, so thanks to Jess, Cath, and Juls. I love you guys.

Thanks, also, to all my friends who helped me grieve my mother's death while I was writing this book. I couldn't have done it without you.

INTRODUCTION

Working with teenagers is one of the most rewarding jobs in the world.[1] Teenagers are energetic, fun, and idealistic; for those of us who connect well with adolescents, working with them is incredibly satisfying. One thing that makes our work so compelling is that adolescence is a time of great intensity. Teenagers have intense thoughts, intense feelings, and intense relationships. There's no denying that adolescence is a dramatic stage of life, and those of us who work with teenagers get swept up in this drama all the time. For the most part, this is what we love about our work. However, occasionally the adolescent drama overwhelms us, and we face incredible challenges in our relationships with teenagers. This is what this book is about, the challenges we experience in our relationships with teens and how we can make sense of them.

Specifically, this book is about the dynamic that occurs between teenagers and adults in schools—or, the teenage world.[2] In my two decades working in schools, first as a teacher and then as a clinician and consultant, I have come to believe that most of the persistent challenges educators face in their work with teens arise from this dynamic. All teachers know their subject area, and they know how to teach, but when it comes to knowing the subject of adolescence many teachers are confused, and rightly so. Teenagers are confusing—they confuse themselves sometimes—so it makes sense that we get confused at times when we deal with them. From hormone surges to fluctuations in brain chemistry to shifting moods, teenagers go through a lot in a day, and therefore it can be hard for them, and us, to keep pace with all the challenges they face.

The truth is teenagers baffled me when I began teaching high school in my mid-twenties, despite the fact that I was practically a teenager myself. I had an advanced degree in education and yet I often felt helpless when faced with an issue that had more to do with adolescence than with what I was trying to teach. Whenever my students did anything typically teenaged, my well-constructed lesson plans went out the window. True, most new teachers face this challenge, but I didn't know much more about adolescence as my experience in the classroom grew. It wasn't until I got training in clinical psychology and social work that I started to get a handle on what was going on with my teenage students. And even then it was hard, much harder than I could have imagined when I began my career.

Even in graduate school, though, I didn't learn anything about my relationship with teenagers. I learned all of the important concepts, such as about the developmental phases of adolescence, but I didn't learn about what was happening to *me* when I dealt with teenagers—and this was what caused me so much confusion. Why did I get so worked up? Why did I act just like them sometimes? Why did I feel so out of control on occasion? I needed answers to these questions and I couldn't find them in any of my textbooks on adolescence. What I did know for sure was that something significant happens in the dynamic between adults and teenagers in schools. That I figured out by myself.

After I left the classroom and became a clinician in schools, I spent a lot of time thinking about this issue and dealing with teachers who struggled with their students in the same way I had. They were puzzled by how to deal with certain aspects of their relationships with teens and they needed guidance and support. As my work with the adults in school communities grew, I realized I needed to think less about traditional adolescent development and more about the dynamic between adults and teens if I wanted to be of service to my colleagues. Thus my adventure began, and this book is the culmination of what I've learned along the way.

My central premise is that adolescence is a profound, potent, and often mysterious process that inevitably affects us in our work with teenagers. This book is about the complex dynamic that is created when we relate to our students who are in the midst of this adolescent process, and how we can make sense of this dynamic. Those of us who work with teens know that adolescence is a force to contend with; it's a force we honor, otherwise we wouldn't teach. But it's also a force that can take us by surprise and put our best-laid plans to rest at a moment's notice.

There's something infectious about adolescence. It can seem almost feverish. Teenage laughter, passion, and *joie de vivre* all conspire to keep us engaged and connected. In this way, I think of adolescence as catching, sort of like a virus, and the positive aspects of adolescence keep us invested in and motivated by our work. Adolescent energy and enthusiasm spread rapidly, and their attention-grabbing message reverberates through the halls of every middle and high school in the land. "We are here! We are here! We are here!" goes the refrain, and we can't ignore it if we try.

Every day those of us who work in schools—teachers, coaches, principals, librarians, you name it—contend with the wonder and perplexity of adolescence, and sometimes the effect it has on us is powerful. We *must* be affected by adolescence in order to do our jobs well, though. Sometimes this effect feels good, as when teenagers inspire us with their enthusiasm or remind us by example of our own idealism. But sometimes it doesn't feel good, as when they frustrate us with their self-absorption or make us impatient with their pettiness. These reactions are normal—all of them, the positive and the negative alike—and naturally we have a wide range of responses to our relationships with our students.

Our relationships with teenagers are complicated as a result, and that's exactly as it should be. We wouldn't get far in the teenage world if we didn't engage, take risks, and get our feet wet in our relationships with our students. Given this degree of investment, our relationships with teens take effort to manage. We must work to establish healthy connections to our students so they feel safe, cared for, and eager to learn. This takes time and attention, and not a little patience, and still the adolescent dynamo surprises us. Nevertheless, this is our job.

To do this job well, teenagers need us to behave like grown-ups. What does this mean? Well, teenagers need us to practice certain skills that allow us to keep our roles clear, to maintain the boundaries between us, and to keep our cool when the energy of adolescence swirls around us. Teenagers need us to be different than they are, and they need us to understand how they affect us, for better or worse. They need us to be healthy, happy, and eager to engage, and they need us to have compassion, for ourselves as much as for them. At the end of the day, teenagers need us to be the best version of ourselves as possible. This is what I mean by *grown-up*.

This book is part primer on adolescent psychology, part primer on adult psychology, and full primer on how adults who work with teenagers can deal with teenagers more effectively. I offer conceptual frameworks that I hope will encourage adults to talk to one another about their work with teens, especially the challenges. I contend that we all face challenges because we all become affected by our teenage students, and therefore we should recognize, acknowledge, and talk about our challenges in an effort to apply best practices in our work.

I also hope that readers use this book as a springboard for contemplation, reflection, and discussion about our relationships in the teenage world. All of us need support in this work because, let's face it, the fever of adolescence can spread at hurricane force at times. I believe the better we understand teenagers and how they operate, the more we protect ourselves from getting blown off course. Also, when we understand our challenges and ourselves, we are free to enjoy our work with teenagers. And isn't that the point?

I use case studies throughout the text to illustrate various aspects of our relationships with teenagers. I have changed all identifying details to protect the identity of the adults and students involved, and in some cases I have created amalgams to highlight specific points. I encourage readers to consider these examples with compassion and care. These stories are *our* stories, and I suspect all of us will see ourselves in these narratives to a greater or lesser degree. This is my wish; that we can examine our work with teenagers with humility and openness and, in the recognition of our shared experience, emerge the better for it.

This book derives as much from my own experiences working with adolescents as it does from my professional observations. I have faltered many times in my relationships with teenagers—more times than I'd like to admit—but each time, I learn something important about myself and about them. Often the lessons aren't clear at first, and sometimes I don't want to learn them, but there they are, waiting for me when I recover my balance.

Finally, if there's one thing I've learned in the course of my career in the teenage world, it's that working with adolescents provides us with endless opportunities to learn, not just to teach.

NOTES

1. I use the terms *teenager* and *adolescent* interchangeably throughout this book, and in both cases I am referring to students from ten to eighteen years of age. True, ten- to twelve-year-olds are not technically teenagers, but many of them have entered puberty and thus have embarked on the process of adolescence. I use these terms to designate students in grades 5–12, with the understanding that there is a huge developmental arc that spans this range.

2. I use the terms *teenage world* and *schools* interchangeably; by *teenage world* I specifically mean middle and high schools. There are many different configurations of schools, so for my purposes the teenage world means schools that teach any subset of grades 5–12.

❶

THE PHENOMENON
OF ADOLESCENCE

Why are teenagers so challenging at times, and why do they get under our skins? In this chapter I explore how teenagers behave and
why they affect others, particularly the adults who work with them
in schools. Since the teenage brain is still developing, teens can't
consistently control their impulses, exercise good judgment, or accurately interpret cues from the external environment. Adults who
work with them must therefore understand how the phenomenon
of adolescence functions and guide teenagers as they navigate their
changing world.

ADOLESCENCE IS CATCHING

Teenagers affect those around them, especially each other. Observe a
group of teenagers in almost any situation and you will see this phenomenon at work: They pick up on each other's cues, react to each other's
moods, and influence each other's ideas (not to mention their choices
in fashion, music, hairstyles, and so on). They are very hard to ignore,
which is partly how they affect adults.

In my twenty years of working with teenagers, I have come to think
of their almost uncanny ability to get under each other's skins, and
under the skins of the adults around them, as being almost infectious.

Teenagers are able to engage us, enrage us, charm us, and disarm us almost instantaneously. This is an incredible skill, when you think about it. Teenagers draw us into their world and change us in the process. This is what I mean when I say adolescence is infectious, even catching. We engage with teenagers and are affected in the process—and that's how it should be.

Given the nature of adolescence, sometimes its effect on us is positive, perhaps thrilling. Adolescence is a time of unbridled enthusiasm and idealism, and often these phenomena infect us. But sometimes it isn't so thrilling. Adolescence is also a time of wild extremes and uncertainty, and sometimes it throws us for a loop. When this happens, we need help to make sense of the situation and to understand our role in the dynamic with our teenage students. When we understand how and why adolescence affects us, we can figure out what to do about it, and this is what this book is about. It's about the phenomenon of adolescence and how it catches us, how it affects our relationships with teenagers, and what we should do when this happens.

SEEKING UNDERSTANDING: LOOKING TO SCIENCE

My understanding of how adolescence catches us, and thus of the dynamic between students and teachers, has been greatly informed by current research about the teenage brain. It is fair to say that this field of inquiry is exploding, and almost every day researchers discover new things about how the teenage brain functions. I believe many of these discoveries can help us better understand why adolescence has an infectious quality to it, and can guide us in our work with teens.

THE TEENAGE BRAIN: SWIMMING WITH SHARKS

Picture this: Three middle school girls are asked the following question. Swimming with sharks: good idea or bad idea?

"Hmmmm . . ." replies the first girl. "Well . . . uhhhhh . . . I guess it would be okay. (Pause) Like, maybe if you did it with someone who did it before. Yeah. Hmmmmmmm . . . (pause). That would be good."

"Yeah," says the second girl, eyes darting back and forth, gauging the reactions of her peers. "It would be a good idea if you went with someone who did it before. (Pause) And maybe if you were in a shark cage."

"Yeah," says the third girl, although with more hesitation than the others. "I guess it would be fine, you know, a good idea. (Pause) Like, if you were in a shark cage with someone who did it before. Yeah, that's okay."

Swimming with sharks? Are they nuts? This was an actual conversation that took place between middle school girls and brain researchers.[1] Furthermore, these girls were smart and well educated. So, what does this interchange tell us about the teenage brain? A lot.

THE TEENAGE BRAIN: A WORK IN PROGRESS

Until recently, scientists believed that the human brain did most of its developing early on and that little changed in the brain after the period of explosive growth that occurs in early childhood. Of course, scientists knew that the brain deteriorated in lots of ways, especially in old age, so no one was saying that the brain didn't change, per se. But as to what happened in the teenage brain in terms of growth, it was assumed to be a non-issue, and therefore of little scientific interest, so science pretty much ignored it.

Advances in technology, in particular in machinery that maps and studies the brain, have changed all that. Science is now paying lots of attention to the teenage brain, and one of the most significant findings is this: The brain is still under construction during adolescence. In fact, the teenage brain is going through a veritable renaissance of growth, almost on par with the initial childhood spurt.

So what does this have to do with swimming with sharks?

The above vignette illustrates a couple of things worth noting about the teenage brain, some of which I'll address later, but most importantly it drives home the point that the teenage brain is really different than the adult brain. Only an adult with impaired cognitive functioning could get away with not knowing that swimming with sharks is a bad idea.

So why do these smart girls, when presented with an admittedly dangerous scenario (they all understood the inherent danger involved, otherwise they wouldn't have qualified their statements the way they did), provide answers capable of sending chills up the adult spine? Because—and we adults must not lose sight of this point—their brains really are different than ours.

HOW THE TEENAGE BRAIN IS DIFFERENT

The biggest difference between teenage and adult brains is what's happening in the front part of the brain, or the frontal lobes, particularly in the prefrontal cortex. This part of the brain regulates *executive functioning*, or those processes that help us reason, control our impulses, formulate sound judgments, and make good decisions. The prefrontal cortex most clearly distinguishes us from other animals and its development is critical.

I like to think of this part of the brain as being like an orchestra; there are many different players (i.e., cognitive functions) whose roles are critical to the brain's overall performance. Ideally, once the brain has matured, the orchestra sounds pretty good; the various players can follow the lead of the conductor and the output is pleasant to listen to.

On the other hand, what happens in the teenage brain sounds like a bad rehearsal sometimes, or the tuning before the conductor has taken the stage. Timing is off in the teenage brain and sometimes the string section is following a different score. You get the picture.

So, the goal of brain development, and the hard work of adolescence, is about bringing all the players into concert and producing a coherent tune. And this takes time.

IT TAKES TIME FOR THE BRAIN TO MATURE

The field of education intuited the development of the teenage brain long before neuroscience took interest. Teachers know a lot about adolescent development, even if they know nothing about neuropsychology. They know, for example, that you can't expect a 7th grader to understand nuance (or even to spell it) the same way a 12th grader can, and that certain abstract concepts are best introduced after a certain age. Teachers understand that even really bright students are limited in how quickly they can grasp certain ideas, and that as educators we must lead and follow the adolescent brain in equal measure.

This new brain research suggests that the human brain continues to develop much longer than even teachers suspected, perhaps somewhere into the mid-twenties. In fact, scientists now believe that the capacity for well-orchestrated executive functioning, especially in the areas of impulse control and risk-taking, may not be fully formed until age twenty-five. (Interestingly, the actuarial field has known this for a long time. This is why in most states you can't rent a car until you're twenty-five.)

The takeaway from this is that we must be mindful always that the brains of our teenage students are different than our own, and that they're changing rapidly. Regardless of how intelligent, on-the-ball, or mature they seem at times, teenage brains have a long way to go.

BACK TO THE SHARKS

Let's return to the girls with the sharks for a moment to explore two functions of the teenage brain that are still under construction. This vignette reveals important things about how the teenage brain reasons and how it is affected, or infected, shall we say, by the opinions of others.

Let's start with the reasoning. We know the girls understand on some level that swimming with sharks is dangerous, or at least not advisable, because they offer qualifications to their responses, like using a shark cage or being with someone who has done it before. But they still can't come up with the correct answer quickly, despite their intelligence. Why? Because in responding to this question they are employing a completely different part of the brain than adults do, and paradoxically, it's the part associated with reasoning.

A brain that has experience and knowledge, and one that has muddled its way through such a scenario before, can respond seemingly instinctively to the shark question. But the teenage brain is grappling with the answer, trying to reason out the various possibilities. It's almost as if the teenage brain has no muscle memory in this department, and therefore it labors over such a task. Whereas the girls came up with the right answer eventually, it took a while, and much longer than it would for an adult brain.

This may give us a clue as to why teenagers don't always learn from the experiences of others, much as we'd like them to. (Those adults who rely on the "When I was a kid" refrain in conversations with teenagers, please take note.)

The second thing about our shark girls is that their answers, facial expressions, eye movements, and body language speak volumes about their relationships to one another. While they are responding, and specifically the two girls who must follow their peer, they are not only reasoning their way through the problem but also trying desperately to evaluate each other's reactions.

We can only imagine the internal dialogue at this point: "What if I say something stupid? What if I say the wrong thing? I want the others to like me, so I can't say something different and risk looking like an idiot." Translation into teenage girl speak: "Oh my God, Oh my God, Oh my God," or something along these lines.

Scientists have discovered that when younger teens, like the shark girls, process emotions, they do not use the frontal cortex as adults do but instead use the amygdala, the reptilian part of the brain that regulates the "fight or flight" response. This means our shark girls are not only straining to answer a question, they're also getting emotionally activated on a very primal level because, in this case, they are doing this mental processing out loud, in front of their peers, and for them this is scary.

Science now reveals that for most girls this age, the prospect of social exclusion or rejection is the most frightening, and therefore the most threatening, thing that can happen. Period. For the shark girls it means that being rejected or shunned, or simply being excluded (which could happen if their responses are not met with approval by their peers), is scarier than anything else that could happen to them, certainly scarier than swimming with sharks, cage or no cage. This is what I mean when I say adolescence is catching.

READING FACIAL EXPRESSIONS: MY TEACHER HATES ME!

The amygdala also plays a role in how teens interpret facial expressions. Rather than using the frontal cortex to make sense of someone's expression, teens employ the amygdala and, as a result, often misinterpret what they see. Imagine that this misinterpretation is coupled with the fight or flight response and you have the recipe for middle school drama. Maybe our shark girls mistakenly see the signs of disdain or anger in the faces of their peers, thus influencing their answers.

This may also account, in part, for adolescent self-absorption. When the teenage amygdala has determined that an expression is hostile (or anything else), the resulting emotional reaction is real. But this doesn't mean it's an accurate read of the situation. To an outside observer, the teen seems to be having an exaggerated or inappropriate response, or both. Now try reasoning with that response. An adult understanding of the situation emerges from a completely different place in the brain than does the teen response, and trying to help a teen understand the "objective" truth can be frustrating, if not futile.

Adults sometimes ask me whether I explain this process to my teenage students, presumably in an effort to help students deal with situations like this or even to prevent them. "Maybe if you told them what was going on in their brains it would help," they suggest. Ah, no.

The truth is, even if teens were interested in their neurological plight on an intellectual level, which is certainly possible, an intellectual understanding wouldn't help them in the moment. To explain the neurological processes involved in their psychological upset would be as effective in resolving the situation as it would be to teach someone to ride a bicycle by using a book. Their brains need practice, not just explanations, and therefore practice over time is the only guaranteed pathway to maturity.

RISKY BUSINESS: KEEPING A LID ON THE ID

This maturity comes at a price, however. To quote Mark Twain, "Good judgment comes from experience. Experience comes from bad judgment."[2] The teenage brain cannot learn only from the experience of others; it must hoe its own row, so to speak. It has to take risks. (Let's hope our shark girls never actually get the opportunity to swim with sharks!)

Of course, *risk* is a relative term here, and each teenage brain calculates risk differently. Nevertheless, all teenagers need to challenge themselves and their brains in order to discover their talents, interests, and limits, and that means taking risks. As we shall see in the next chapter, this is a charged subject for adults, and it is in the area of teenage risk that the phenomenon of adolescence can wreak the most havoc in the adult-teen relationship.

One trend I have noticed over the course of my career is the increasing hesitation on the part of adults, parents and teachers alike, to let kids take risks. Teachers, of course, understand the need for teens to take intellectual risks. This is at the core of good teaching and teachers know that students get much more out of learning if there is some—but not too much—risk involved. When it comes to physical and emotional risks, however, it's as though this culture has put a wet blanket over its children, all in the name of safety, fairness, and being nice.

What science tells us now is that the brain learns, in part, by taking risks, and while adults must stay involved and help the teenage brain calculate these risks, teens must take risks on their own. And when they take risks, teenagers will make mistakes, get hurt, occasionally hurt others, and fail, all in the name of development.

This can be a terrifying prospect for adults who work with teens, yet it is reality. Teens need to learn how to control their impulses, which drive their risk-taking behaviors, and adults need to help them do this. As Freud might say, teens need to put a lid on the id.[3] When teenagers can't do this for themselves, adults must be the lid for them (more on this later).

This is a big part of what makes dealing with teenagers so challenging. Ask any new teacher about classroom management and you'll get an idea about how challenging it can be. The stakes are high and sometimes dangerous as the teen brain learns how to orchestrate its desires, impulses, and thoughts, but all of this is necessary for healthy development.

IMITATION: FLATTERY OR CHEMISTRY?

One hallmark of adolescence is the herd mentality, which explains why nearly every student at the last school I worked at wore Ugg boots and North Face jackets. We now know that the teenage brain learns through imitation, and given the importance of peer relationships during adolescence, this explains, in part, why the herd mentality often grips groups of teens.

A central psychological task of this stage of life is identity formation, and affiliation to groups or causes is one way this plays out for teens. Identity in adolescence is ever-shifting, too, so the average teen may switch friendships, group affiliation, clothes and hairstyles, and even speech patterns often in an effort to discover his or her "real" self.

This propensity for imitation makes the prospect of peer pressure and influence very real, and whatever good judgment exists in the teen brain may be trumped by bad judgment in a group of peers. The good news is that teens don't imitate just peers, although peers are often kept in higher regard than adults. The teen brain is imitating and thus learning from all kinds of sources, including adult teachers.

A small percentage of teens seem to have an immunity to herd mentality and thus to peer pressure, which may have something to do with how their brains function, possibly their amygdalas. These students are rare, though, and they shouldn't be confused with students who imitate by being opposed to prevailing trends. Teens who present themselves as countercultural are just as affected by their peers as those who stay with the herd, perhaps even more so. But a few teenagers really are different.

In my experience, students who naturally can resist the pressure to conform to their peers don't display the same moodiness or insecurity as other teens do. I used to think this had to do exclusively with parenting, but I'm not so sure it does. I once asked the father of such a student how he managed to raise his even-keeled and independent daughter. "Don't ask me," he said. "I have no idea where she came from."

Someday I suspect scientists will figure out where kids like this come from but until they do, and until they develop a pill to help the rest of the herd, the group mentality of adolescence is here to stay.

FROM CROTCH TO PREFRONTAL CORTEX AND BACK

It used to be that adolescence was associated with one thing and one thing only: hormones. This shift in focus from the crotch to the frontal lobes is new, but research on the teenage brain doesn't mean hormones don't play a big part of the phenomenon of adolescence. Hormones change the body—transforming it from child to adult—fuel the sex drive, and contribute to the moodiness that is so characteristic of adolescence.

Thus hormones play a big role in how adults are affected by teenagers, a topic I will address in the next chapter. So while science continues to discover new things about the teenage brain, there remain some things we've known forever.

NAVIGATING TWO WORLDS: BARBIE DOLLS TO CONDOMS

Given the massive changes taking place for teenagers, from the microscopic ones happening in the brain to the macroscopic ones happening in the body, it's surprising teens function as well as they do. I often say to adults that if we went through as many changes as teenagers do in the course of a week, we'd feel crazy too.

The ultimate challenge teens must master in the face of all these incremental changes is how to make the transition from childhood to adulthood. This transition can take a decade or more to complete, so for years adolescents are navigating two realities—or going back and forth between Barbie dolls and condoms, as one astute teacher once put it.

Adolescents are at times worldly and naïve, knowledgeable and ignorant, confident and scared. They are standing on ground that is constantly shifting and often they are at a loss to know which world they inhabit. Their moments of insight and triumph are followed without fail by ones of confusion and chaos, and finding the center is often an elusive goal.

But in the end this is their task: to discover who they are and who they want to be, and for them the discoveries of science are meaningless. It is *our* job to understand what they are going through and to help them make sense of their journey.

THE DEVELOPMENTAL SPECTRUM

One way to do this is to understand that the journey of adolescence unfolds and progresses over time and it can't be rushed. As I stated earlier, 7th graders and seniors are very different animals, and even a thirteen-year-old genius does not fit in developmentally with a group of 12th graders. Teachers know this instinctively. To this end, most teachers have a preference for dealing with students at a certain stage on the developmental spectrum. It is rare to find a teacher who likes to work equally with all levels of adolescents (grades 5–12). Regardless of our preferences, we should be aware of some of the major developmental changes that occur throughout adolescence so that we can understand where our students are coming from, where they're going, and when they've lost their way.

The following is a brief overview[4] of four stages of adolescent development:

1. Early Middle School (Grades 5 and 6)
2. Late Middle School (Grades 7 and 8)
3. Early High School (Grades 9 and 10)
4. Late High School (Grades 11 and 12)

We should all acquaint ourselves with this developmental spectrum and be well versed in our area of concentration. Knowledge is power, and therefore we need a lot of knowledge to deal with our teenage students.

1. Early Middle School, Grades 5 and 6

Many kids, especially girls, start puberty[5] during this time, although some begin earlier or later. As their bodies change and grow, students start to become more self-conscious and aware of their surroundings. They also become more moody, and this is when teachers sense the end of childhood and the beginning of adolescence in their students. For the most part, though, students at this age are more childlike than adolescent, and this is very true in terms of how they think.

Fifth and 6th graders are still concrete thinkers and they are just beginning to develop the skills that will allow them to reason, organize, and execute complex cognitive functions. Their executive functioning is not well developed at this stage and they need lots of oversight when it comes to staying on task. Peers are important but kids are not hyper-reactive to their classmates. In one sense, the herd is not fully formed yet. The agony of peer pressure has not peaked at this stage and students can actually tolerate differences a little better than they will be able to in a few years time. Kids at this age feel very connected to and identify with their parents and teachers. The quest for separation has not yet begun in earnest.

Teachers who like this stage of development tend to prefer working hands-on with students and place a high value on the close relationship they can forge with students. They like working with kids, not teens, and often the developmentally precocious student is a headache for these teachers.

2. Late Middle School, Grades 7 and 8

I call late middle school the era of Drama and Trauma. Puberty has begun for most students and mood swings, awkward gaits, orthodontia, acne, and poor personal hygiene are the norm. It is during this time that schools often mediate one of the first rights of passage of adolescence, the school dance. The pain of self-consciousness and the herd mentality can be studied in depth at such functions.

During the late middle school years, students make huge strides in their capacity to reason, with many kids being able to grasp complex subjects like algebra by the end of the 8th grade. They can think a little bit outside the box as their capacity for abstraction begins, but executive functioning is still limited in most kids. Social development and awareness is all consuming during this phase, and even the nicest student may turn into a backstabbing gossip or schoolyard bully with little provocation. This is normal, albeit undesirable from an adult perspective.

The fight or flight response is particularly active during this stage. Social situations, especially those that involve inclusion and exclusion, cause the brain to work overtime. Most students have trouble reading social cues at this age and all kids feel left out or victimized at some point during this period. This is why adults tend to place so much emphasis on concepts like cooperation, fairness, and safety during this time, because kids often feel left out, slighted, and socially unsafe.

Teachers who prefer this age group tend to like the energy, blossoming intellect, and relatively uncomplicated social issues that prevail (by less complicated, I mean most kids this age are not involved with sex or drugs and are not driving cars yet). Generally, they like to be involved in most aspects of their students' experience. Teachers at this stage have a profound impact on students, and students are usually willing to acknowledge their affection for and dependence on their teachers.

3. Early High School, Grades 9 and 10

By early high school, most students are well into puberty and identify themselves as adolescents, not as children. Some of the cattiness of middle school has subsided by this time but the herd mentality prevails. Teens in early high school remain very self-conscious and preoccupied with what their peers think of them, and a social *faux pas* can cause them great distress. Cognitively, they are entering a new world, one where teachers expect them to think and reason less like children and more like adults, and their brains have to keep pace with these new demands.

This can be a difficult challenge, and teachers must remember that it takes time for the teenage brain to coordinate all the tasks it needs to accomplish. Many teens at the beginning of high school may not be able to organize themselves or their work effectively and must be guided and taught how to keep track of multiple and long-term assignments. The leap from 8th to 9th grade is big in this regard, and the teenage brain needs assistance to pull together the various pieces of the puzzle. Ninth graders may have to be told again and again how to take notes, remember their assignments, and follow through with their work. This is not teenage delinquency but rather the developing capacity for executive functioning at work, and teens need help from their teachers to meet the increased expectations placed on them.

As their cognitive world gets more complicated, so too does their social world. Self-awareness, self-absorption, and the importance of peer relationships increase during this time, but most teenagers say they feel better about themselves than they did in middle school. They are still at the mercy of their peers, though, and as they begin to separate from the opinions of adults, they increase the value they place on the opinion of their peers. By the end of 10th grade, the search for identity is in full force. I call this the Hamlet stage, wherein teens start to ask themselves the essential questions about their life's purpose and their reason for being.

Teenagers at this stage tend to be idealistic, eager, fairly naïve, and relatively innocent. In relation to 11th and 12th graders, they can seem almost childlike. Teachers who like this stage of development tend to enjoy helping students make the transition into more mature thinking and watching them become aware of the larger world around them.

4. Late High School, Grades 11 and 12

Most teenagers by late high school have bodies that function like adult ones, even as their size and shape continue to change. Their brains have developed and many teens at this stage can display almost adult-like maturity periodically. Smart teens can think abstractly by this point and can handle very complicated intellectual tasks.

By late high school, most teens enjoy a lessening of mood swings, and when they get moody they have developed some skill and experience to deal with their emotional ups and downs. They can see the world in more than black and white terms. This doesn't mean their inner experiences don't affect them, just that they have begun to develop the capacity to recognize and regulate what's going on inside.

Social relationships get both easier and more complicated during this time. Most teens at this stage say they feel less pressured by friends than they used to but the risks they take are higher. Whereas in middle school the pressure might be to wear certain clothes, now the pressure might be to have sex or to ride with someone who has been drinking. Factors like alcohol, driving, and sex up the risk ante during this stage, and the teenage brain sometimes displays appalling judgment relative to its responsibilities and the expectations placed upon it.

Teachers who prefer this stage of development tend to like relating to students as adults and not as children. Teachers like the fact that they can converse with late high school students without a lot of distraction, and they appreciate that by this age teenagers have a lot of control over their impulses: They can sit still and focus on the task at hand. Students prepare to launch into the "real" world during this time, and teachers enjoy helping them get ready for this rite of passage. Bright students in late high school can be very intellectually savvy and exciting to work with, and they can see beyond their own horizons and appreciate the perspective of others.

By the time teenagers graduate from high school, their brains have developed into well-reasoning and semi-reliable entities and they are ready to live without constant adult supervision and guidance, for the most part. They are no longer in the constant grip of the adolescent brain and they can function reasonably well in the adult world. Even the most obstinate or oppositional teenage brain develops over time (exceptions exist, of course), as the capacity for executive functioning, mood regulation, and insight increases.

WHAT'S THE POINT: DO ADULTS MAKE A DIFFERENCE?

If all this brain development is inevitable, do adults make a difference in the lives of teenagers?

It would be a mistake to conclude from this new research on the teenage brain that teens are simply neurological events encased in changing bodies. While it is true that certain aspects of neurological development define the teenage experience, teenagers are more than the sum of their cognitive parts, and therefore their developmental challenges should not be viewed exclusively through the lens of neuroscience. To do so is to reduce them to mere processes and functions, and we all know teens are more than that. So, while science helps us to understand what's going on in the teen brain, it's merely one way to understand adolescence.

While acknowledging the importance of science, we also must make room for the importance of relationship, and specifically the relationship between teens and adults in schools. One teacher, after hearing me lecture about the teenage brain and sensing the inevitability of neurological development, asked, "Do we matter at all?"

This is a great question, perhaps the most important question I've ever been asked. The answer, of course, is a resounding *yes*. Teachers not only matter, they make all the difference in the world. The teenage brain cannot grow in isolation; it needs to be challenged, cared for, disciplined, and taught. It needs everything from us, which is why it is so important for us to understand the phenomenon of adolescence.

Teens need more from us than we, or they, can imagine, despite their protests to the contrary (imagine our shark girls without the guidance of adults). Teachers play a critical role in teenage development, and let's not forget it.

IT'S NOT MY JOB, OR IS IT?

It is so important for adults who work in the teenage world to understand the ways in which teenagers affect us, because it is our job to help teenagers grow up, not just to learn math or science or French. I bet not one teacher reading this book was questioned about this aspect of the job during an interview. You probably were not asked about child rearing or discipline or about the roles adults play in the lives of their teenage students. And yet these may be the most critical aspects of our work with teenagers, whether we understand them or not.

Knowing our subject area is only half of our job, and maybe not even the most important half. We must also know the contents of our teenage subjects—how their brains functions, how they affect each other, and most importantly, how they affect us. Understanding these things helps us immeasurably in our work. In fact, it makes the work possible. If we don't understand teenagers and our relationships with them, we can't really help them grow up and we aren't really doing our jobs.

Some teachers don't think it should be our responsibility to help teenagers grow up. This is what parents are for, they reason, and they argue that to assume such responsibility is to overstep our bounds. I understand this argument, and I'm not suggesting we assume parental responsibilities with our students, but I am suggesting that it is our job to get involved with our students beyond delivering our lesson plans. Luckily, this happens naturally when teenagers get under our skins. The truth is we can't escape our relationship with students, and it is within the context of these relationships that we help them grow up. So perhaps the most important thing we can do to help our teenager students is to recognize how they affect us.

This is why we matter so much—because we affect teenagers and teenagers affect us—and this is what this book is about.

EXERCISES AND REFLECTIONS

To understand the phenomenon of adolescence, we must recognize the ways teenagers affect each other and us. The following exercises are designed to help us explore our relationship with our teenage students and our work in the teenage world.

I suggest you consider each exercise on your own and then, if possible, share your thoughts with one or more colleagues. In my experience, teachers can learn a lot from each other. I can guarantee that at least one of your colleagues needs to hear what you have to say about these issues, so please consider initiating a conversation with a fellow educator as part of this process of exploration.

1. List three things you like about working with teenagers. Why? List three things you don't like. Why? Describe how you came to teach adolescents.
2. The frontal lobe of the teenage brain is a work in progress. Cognitive functions such as judgment, reasoning, impulse control, and attention are not fully established until the mid-twenties. Describe a situation with a student(s) that occurred recently in your classroom (or at your school) that illustrates the lack of development of one or more of these cognitive functions. What happened? What was your reaction?
3. What are some of the major social trends among students at your school? This could include fashion, political persuasions, clubs, sports, etc. How do teens pressure each other at your school?
4. What standards of behavior have teenagers established for themselves and each other in your school community? What degree of influence do adults have over teenagers at your school?
5. How are adults treated by teens in your school community? Do you feel you get the respect you desire/deserve as an educator? What balance exists between the adult and teenage worlds in your school and who sets the tone?
6. A group of students is making noise in the hallway during a break between classes. The group quickly gets loud and out of control. You do not teach or know any of the students involved. How are you expected to respond at your school? How do you respond?
7. You overhear a group of students bad-mouthing a fellow teacher. What is your reaction? How are you expected to deal with a situation like this at your school?
8. Recall a time when you felt you lost control of a situation with students. What happened? What aspect of the phenomenon of adolescence affected you? In retrospect, does your response seem appropriate, or can you think of a more effective response to the situation?

CHAPTER SUMMARY

Teenagers have a profound effect on those around them. Adults who work in schools, or in the teenage world, should understand how the phenomenon of adolescence operates in an effort to be effective in their work with teenagers. Teenagers need adults to guide them as they make sense of their changing worlds because their brains are still under construction, therefore adults must recognize how they become affected in their relationships with teens.

NOTES

1. Data presented by Abigail Baird, Ph.D., Assistant Professor of Psychology, Vassar College, at Learning and the Brain Conference, Cambridge, MA, 2005. Conversation reconstructed by author.

2. There is some debate about the attribution of this quote, however, many people consider Mark Twain to be its author.

3. Freud used the term *id* to describe unconscious human drives, particularly sex and aggression.

4. When I say this is a *brief* overview, I mean it. It's brief, and therefore it should not be considered comprehensive or authoritative. There are many books available for educators on child and adolescent development, some of which I include in the references section.

5. The term *puberty* describes the physical changes that take place during adolescence.

2

ADULTS IN THE HOT ZONE: WORKING IN THE TEENAGE WORLD

Adults who work in the teenage world are in a veritable hot zone of the phenomenon of adolescence and there is no way to avoid getting affected by it. In this chapter I use case studies to illustrate the various ways this can happen, and to underscore that relationships between adults and teenagers in schools are complicated, never reciprocal, and provide valuable information to adults about their own psychology.

LOCATION, LOCATION, LOCATION: WORKING IN THE HOT ZONE

Most adults spend their days either with other adults or with their own children. Not so with teachers. Teachers spend their days with interaction limited to children and other people's children, and many of these children are teenagers. When you put it this way, the job of teaching sounds almost crazy. Who would want to spend time with other people's teenagers? All day? Every day?

The next time you are with non-teacher adults, ask them if they would willingly spend lots of time with other people's teenagers. The kindest response you will get is something along the lines of, "Oh, no. I could never do that, but thank goodness there are people like you in the world." It is more likely that your question will elicit eye rolling and a response such as, "Are you kidding me? Not a chance. I can barely stand my own teenagers."

It is not, I repeat *not*, crazy to work with teenagers, and those of us who love to teach know this. But the reaction of many adults to the prospect of spending time with teens is evidence that the effect teenagers have on others is real. Most adults want to avoid it at all cost. Thankfully, teachers don't, but we should be aware of what we're getting into when we agree to immerse ourselves in the teenage world.

If adolescence has an infectious quality to it, as I suggested in chapter 1, then schools are the *hot zones* of the phenomenon. Adolescence is in its most concentrated form in schools, especially the aspects that involve herd mentality, imitation, peer pressure, and so on. As I like to remind adults, school is a teenager's whole life, as opposed to just a place to go during the day. School is where teenagers socialize with friends, fall in love, get their hearts broken, discover who they are, connect to the world. School is where everything or practically everything happens. As a result, the phenomenon of adolescence permeates schools. Schools are veritable petri dishes swarming with the adolescent fever.

This presents a challenge for those of us who work in schools. For us, school is work, not life, or at least that's what it's supposed to be. But to do our work we must enter a hot zone of feverish activity that has little to do with us, except for the undeniable fact that it's our job to deal with it.

THE PARALLEL CURRICULUM

As I noted earlier, some of us resist the notion that it is our responsibility to do anything more than teach and perform whatever other activities we have agreed to contractually (go yearbook staff!). Why should we worry about this other stuff, like how teenagers affect us? It's not in our job description. True that, as my students would say. But as any experienced teacher can attest, knowing one's subject matter is not enough when it comes to doing the job, and teaching content is only a small part of what good educators do.

In order to be effective with teens, adults need to know all kinds of things about the dynamic nature of adolescence, like how to calm down the hysterical student who just had a fight with her best friend, how to break up a fight in the hallway, or how to deal with the heartbreak of the student who never gets picked as a lab partner. This is what I call the parallel curriculum, and there's one for students and adults alike.

For students, the parallel curriculum is the real work of adolescence. It's about growing up, discovering their voice, making sense of the world, managing frustration, and accepting who they are. It is the work of dealing with adolescence in its most florid state, and it can be brutal. Given the developmental challenges on the teenage plate, it's a wonder they learn anything at all in the classroom.

For those who don't remember adolescence and can't recall the horror, let me remind you of how difficult it is to concentrate when you are attracted to the person sitting next to you, or walk through a cafeteria with perspiration stains on your shirt, or are left out of a social event. Add to this the pain of making a mistake in front of your peers, which is what teens risk every day in the classroom, and you can see how hard this work really is.

What adults dismiss as petty annoyance, teenagers are held hostage to, and their work, at times, is to simply survive the day. The parallel curriculum is unavoidable. Teenagers can't drop a course or advance to the next level without going through all the phases of the curriculum, many of them painful.

The parallel curriculum for adults begins with the recognition that the parallel curriculum for students is real. It cannot be minimized, at least not in the minds and brains of the teenagers themselves and therefore we shouldn't minimize it either. We should take the phenomenon of adolescence and the parallel curriculum seriously if we want to really understand our students.

This is an awesome mandate—and who knew? How many of us were advised of the parallel curriculum and this added responsibility before entering the teaching profession? None that I know of. I know I wasn't. Lack of full disclosure notwithstanding, we must understand this responsibility if for no other reason than to do otherwise means to let our colleagues and students down. The truth is someone has to help bring down the fever of adolescence in schools because teenagers can't do it themselves. So, it's up to the adults to do it, every single one of us.

NOBODY IS IMMUNE

One common method of dealing with the vicissitudes of adolescence is to deny its effect on us. I know of adults who believe they can slip in and out of the teenage world every day and remain unmoved by the experience. Others imagine it is possible to pick and choose which aspects of adolescence they deal with. I know this experience well. I have been there myself.

Unfortunately, these methods of coping don't work, but this doesn't stop most of us from employing them on occasion. I think denial is our effort to imagine we have immunity to our teenage students; it is a comforting thought. But it's a lie. None of us is immune.

What does this really mean, though? If none of us is immune from the influence of our teenage students, then what does it look like when we get affected, or infected, by them? Think of it this way: The phenomenon of adolescence has a viral quality to it and viruses penetrate boundaries. Viruses disregard the rules. They invade our space without our knowledge or consent. Therefore, to be infected by adolescence means to have our boundaries crossed and to have the teenage world enter our own. It means being affected by the moods, energy, and general chaos of the adolescent world. In sum, it means working with teenagers.

WHAT INFECTION LOOKS LIKE

Here's an example I like to use to illustrate what infection looks like. But before I continue, let me say that each of us reacts to teenagers differently. Every adult brings to the teaching profession his or her own set of experiences and skills, and different resistances and vulnerabilities as a result; therefore, one person's heightened response is another person's indifference to the effect teenagers have on us.

Now, to the example. I was asked to consult with a middle school where some troublesome behavior was occurring among a group of 7th grade girls. The faculty and administration wanted advice on how to deal with the situation, and so I met with all of the parties involved.

One girl was feeling very targeted by some classmates, a group considered the "mean" girls. She complained of being excluded and overhearing gossip about herself that included charges of sexual promiscuity.

She believed the "mean" girls were harassing her and, not surprisingly, she wanted the harassment to stop.

The "mean" girls, meanwhile, were clear in their dislike of this girl. This point was beyond dispute; they readily admitted they didn't like this girl. But beyond the admission that the "mean" girls didn't like their classmate, they didn't admit to any of the other charges and no adult had observed any of the bad behavior that was being reported by the victim in question. This left the adults feeling helpless about how to right the wrongs they believed were being perpetrated.

The adults tried the standard approaches of intervention: They talked to the "perpetrators" and explained to them that their behavior was wrong (even though they couldn't really pinpoint the behavior); they had a class discussion about bullying; and they even contacted all of the parents in the 7th grade to inform them of the behavior.

Okay, so far we have a typical middle school scenario, one that plays out daily in schools across the country. Except for one thing. Some of the faculty in this case, all experienced, dedicated, thoughtful teachers, were calling for an expulsion from school of the "mean" girls. Without one shred of evidence of rule breaking or bad behavior, they wanted to see these girls expelled from school. One teacher even said she thought the girls should face legal charges of harassment.

Now, how is this an example of infection by adolescence? On the face of it, the behavior in question among the girls was mild. In fact, I would not have termed it bullying myself, however, that's how the school labeled it. To me it was typical unpleasant, middle school behavior (believe me, I have seen horrible bullying behavior and this was not it). All of the kids involved were good kids, all of them.

What was happening among the students was a poignant example of what happens in the misfiring, not-fully-developed teenage brain as it tries to navigate social situations. True, feelings were getting hurt, people were being excluded, and no one was winning congeniality awards, not even the targeted girl, but the behavior was typical and mild (which is not to say that it should have been ignored; something needed to be done especially to support the girl who was being targeted).

However, what was happening among the adults was anything but mild. It was seething. It was nasty. It was totally irrational. In a word, it was adolescent. I heard middle-aged adults call for the public humiliation of twelve-year-old girls. I saw adults literally shake their fists at colleagues who disagreed with their view of the situation. I heard rumors and gossip and witnessed backbiting comments, all in the name of protecting students. Finally, and perhaps most disturbingly, I heard adults say things about students that were far worse than the alleged comments that got the ball rolling in the first place.

This is what it looks like to get caught in the grip of the phenomenon of adolescence, and in this case the grip was pretty tight. The adults in question were behaving in the exact same way as their students; in fact their behavior was much more problematic because presumably their brains were fully developed. But before I shake my fist too strongly at these teachers, let me underscore that this happens to *all of us* at times in the teenage world. All of us.

What happened to these teachers was not their fault, per se, but it was their responsibility to understand what was going on and to extricate themselves from the situation. This is what all of us must do in our work with teenagers. When we are drawn into the teenage drama, we must recognize the drama for what it is and evaluate our role in the play. This case illustrates that sometimes it's hard to step back from a feverish situation and make sense of the circumstances in the moment, and sometimes we act before we think and render judgment too quickly. This is how the teenage brain behaves, and when we're immersed in the teenage world sometimes our brains respond in kind.

How did this happen in this particular instance? How did these good and well-intentioned teachers get so caught up in the situation?

First, all of the adults felt troubled by the alleged behavior. It was clear the targeted student was in pain. Her emotional response to the situation was typical for her age: She was weepy and sullen, even raw. She broke down in front of a number of teachers, and so various adults witnessed in person the pain she suffered. Remember, if you will, that the threat of social exclusion is the scariest event for a girl this age, so this experience was excruciating for the targeted girl. The teachers naturally felt sympathy for her and responded to her subjective experience of exclusion and pain, which was valid. But because of their strong feelings of sympathy, they overlooked the broader situation, which had many different story lines and which was equally valid.

Second, this was a school that prided itself on the behavior of its students. The school saw itself as having only "good kids." The margin of error for student behavior was small as a result, so even run-of-the-mill adolescent misbehavior stood out. For their part, teachers were not used to dealing with the darker side of the adolescent psyche; they tended to not see this as part of their job because, in their minds, their students were "good." This attitude is common. All schools want to see themselves as having good kids, and for the most part all schools *do* have good kids, just as this one did. But even good teenagers have brains that misfire, and we must allow for this reality. More important, we must allow for the reality that sometimes we get swept up in the teenage drama, and when we do it's harder for us to evaluate the situation on its merits.

Third, my guess is that many of the teachers involved gauged their own performance in part on their students' behavior, and therefore when their students' behavior didn't conform to their expectations, they saw this as a reflection of their worthiness as teachers. In their minds, good students equaled good teachers, and vice versa, and therefore they took "bad" student behavior personally. They also felt frustrated and helpless, something we all fall prey to in our work, especially when we see our students suffer and we can't seem to fix the situation. The teachers in this case experienced many of the same emotions the targeted student felt, which is precisely my point. Once these feelings overtook them, they viewed the situation personally and lost their perspective.

Fourth, on a personal level, a number of these teachers were quick to identify themselves with the targeted student. They felt marginalized in their lives for various reasons, and as a result, it took them longer to separate their own experiences from those of their students, at least in this case. Their personal vulnerabilities meshed well with what was happening among the students, and therefore they identified with the situation as it played out.

All of the teachers in this situation were committed to doing their best but some of them were caught up in the heightened emotions of the moment. They saw the situation through one student's eyes and lost sight of the larger perspective. Their impassioned responses stemmed also from legitimate but unrelated experiences of their own, many of which had roots reaching down to their own middle school experiences. As these adults called for the excoriation and expulsion of the twelve-year-old girls, they were exorcising their own demons.

This is how we can get caught up in the adolescent whirlwind. Circumstances conspire to create situations wherein we have difficulty separating our own inner experiences from the matter at hand. In this case, the adults matched their students' emotionality and drama, point for point. They took sides, saw things as black or white, and had trouble acknowledging the larger picture. A small flame, sparked by a few girls, exploded into a conflagration among faculty that threatened to scorch the earth. Ironically, in the midst of the turmoil, the adults lost sight of the fact that their students, all of them, really were good kids, just as they wanted them to be. But the brains of good teenagers are still under construction and this sort of nasty behavior is one of the results.

ADOLESCENCE IS SORT OF LIKE A VIRUS

It would be easy to judge the above-mentioned teachers' behavior as being overwrought, but that would be a mistake. Their feelings and re-actions to the situation were real, and yet those emotions threatened to overtake the moment and cause everyone to lose sight of the students' needs. A more helpful approach is to consider the situation in light of the viral metaphor. In this case, the phenomenon of adolescence be-haved sort of like a virus. The feverish intensity and contagious nature of the adolescent drama infected the teachers. Given this particular school and these particular adults, infection was inevitable. It's worth repeating that it wasn't the adults' fault they got so exercised in the moment, but it was their responsibility to do something about it. It was their job to contain the situation.

The thing I love about using the viral metaphor to explain the dy-namics between teenagers and the adults who work with them is that it normalizes the kinds of things that happen all the time in schools, and it gets us off the hook from feeling guilty, and thus paralyzed, when we make mistakes. If we work in the teenage world, we all are infected and caught off guard at times by the adolescent fever, just like these adults were. (For the record, not all of the adults involved in this case reacted with such intensity. For some of them, this situation wasn't charged, and so they weren't thrown off course. Nevertheless, they were in a hot zone and still had to deal with the situation.)

The viral metaphor also provides a conceptual framework for what happens in the moment. The simple act of identifying the process can be a powerful form of containment. Adults who understand the nature of adolescence, and how it affects adults and their particular vulnerability to the teenage fever, are able to get perspective quickly, which serves to reduce the fever immediately. Again, while none of us is immune from being affected by our relationship with teenagers, each of us is responsible for making sense of the dynamic and getting ourselves back on track.

The adults in this scenario needed to look at their own reactions before they could be helpful to their students. They needed to figure out what was pushing their buttons and determine how they were contributing to the situation. They needed to exercise the cognitive functions that their students couldn't yet employ (at least not on a regular basis), namely impulse control, reasoning, empathy, and good judgment.

In essence, they needed to understand that they had been infected by the feverish nature of adolescence; acknowledge that their personal reactions were contributing to the situation and to the functioning of the group as a whole; and take care of themselves.

This is the work of the parallel curriculum, and it can be difficult.

YOU'LL NEVER NEED THERAPY AGAIN

When I address new teachers about working with teenagers, I tell them that their students can identify their vulnerabilities faster than the speed of light. They can target their feelings of insecurity, weakness, and fear almost instantly. This is what it means to be affected by the phenomenon of adolescence in the teenage world.

I give this talk only to adults who have had the chance to experience what I'm talking about. Saying this to someone who hadn't yet worked with teenagers would be daunting, I think, and it could turn him or her off teaching. But to adults with even a few weeks of experience working with teens, these statements are met with nods of recognition.

These folks know that teenagers, especially groups of teens, push buttons. I tell new teachers if they're interested in getting in touch with their deepest fears and phobias, teaching teens is the profession for them. They'll never again have to rely on a therapist to unearth their "issues." Their students will take care of that for them, free of charge. (Of course, once these issues are unearthed they may need a therapist, but that's another matter.)

New teachers sometimes ask me when they can expect to be finished with all this business. The answer is never, really. As the previous example illustrates teachers at any stage of development are drawn into the teenage drama. As we grow into ourselves as professionals, we learn how to manage the adolescent fever and our reactions to it better but we never reach a point of completion. This is good news for all of us, though, because it means we must stay engaged and aware in our relationships with our students. As we do, we also continue to progress on our personal learning curve long after we've mastered the pedagogical one.

The parallel curriculum for adults, then, has a developmental quality to it, just like the one for students. New teachers have different vulnerabilities than experienced teachers but, again, every adult is unique.

The following are more examples of how adults get affected in their work with teenagers and what our own parallel curriculum consists of.

The Case of Alex

Alex was a relatively young, new teacher and a freshly minted Ph.D. who hadn't spent any time out of school herself. She was an instant hit in the classroom, in part because she had lots of experience teaching from her graduate school days. She was also conscientious, hard working, and responsive, and parents and colleagues alike told the administration how pleased they were with this new hire.

Alex was assigned to chaperone the first school dance and when she asked her colleagues what to expect, she was given little guidance about her role. As a result, when she was invited to dance by one of her students she didn't know what to do and so, caught off guard, she said yes. Soon a group of students had circled around and were encouraging her to continue dancing. The students were not making fun of Alex. They saw her as young and cool and much more interesting than their other teachers. Everyone was having a good time, Alex included.

That first chaperone experience was followed by the homecoming dance, then the semi-formal, then the spring fling, and Alex was still dancing. The students had designated songs that were hers and a ritual developed around Alex and her participation in these events. It should be noted that at no time did Alex receive any feedback or advice from her fellow chaperones. The phenomenon of adolescence was left to flourish on everyone's watch, and Alex got caught in the crossfire.

For Alex, school dances started to be important. The first one left her feeling validated and accepted, things she hadn't felt during high school. By paying attention to her, Alex's students provided her with an experience she'd never had before, and so slowly, over the course of time, Alex no longer participated in the dances as a chaperone. After a while, she was there as a glorified student.

Alex had not set out to become the focus of attention at the dances. Nor had she gone into teaching, at least not consciously, in an effort to have reparative experiences. But that's what happened. Alex's situation is very common for new teachers, especially young teachers who are closer in age to their students than to most of their colleagues. It can feel intoxicating to receive so much attention, and when students provide positive feedback about certain behaviors, we are vulnerable to repeat these behaviors. If no one is there to help give direction in the situation, young or inexperienced teachers are apt to absorb the drama, just as Alex did.

In this situation, Alex needed the help of an experienced adult to extricate her from the situation, and then to discuss with her how to avoid similar dilemmas in the future. Alex's popularity and appeal were not going to wane just because she stopped dancing. In fact, now that she had set a precedent, the pressure on her from students to join in with them was probably going to increase. Alex was on a slippery slope, and a seasoned adult within the community needed to help her develop a strategy to stay connected to her students without putting herself on the line.

Common signs of getting caught in the snare of adolescence are the potent feelings adults experience at the hands of their students, like intoxication as a result of inclusion, or devastation as a result of exclusion. There is nothing more powerful than being on the inside of a system that values inclusion above all else, as was true in Alex's case. On the other hand, there is nothing worse than being made to feel invisible. This is Dave's story.

The Case of Dave

Dave had taught at the same school for decades and, for many years, he was beloved by his students. He was elected to speak at graduation twice and had the yearbook dedicated to him a number of times. He was very popular, and he loved it. But as he got older, Dave noticed a change in his relationship to his students. Few clustered around his desk after class anymore. Fewer still elected him to advise clubs or mentor their independent projects. As time passed, Dave remained an effective teacher in the classroom but he couldn't help notice how outdated he felt. While it was true that he was still liked by his students, his time as the chosen one was over.

Dave took this change in status hard. It felt like he got kicked out of the popular group, which is kind of what happened. Without a certain type of recognition from his students, Dave felt deflated and depressed. He'd never realized how much he depended on their approbation to bolster his feelings of self-worth as a teacher and as a person, and without it he wasn't sure he wanted to keep teaching.

After years of being in the "in" crowd, Dave was feeling the effects of exclusion. He'd been dumped and he knew it. Unfortunately for Dave, the power of adolescent adoration had kept him going, so much so that he'd never had to consider what other aspects of his job gave him meaning and satisfaction. When he got the boot from his students, he felt helpless and lost, just like teenagers do much of the time.

An astute administrator could have helped Dave deal with his dilemmas; he needed guidance from someone in a position to lend perspective to his situation. An experienced administrator could have anticipated his needs, as his scenario exemplifies a common challenge faced by seasoned teachers, particularly the popular ones. Dave needed help to deal with his changing role vis-à-vis his students as he grew older, and he needed to find ways to stay invested in his work now that he wasn't the flavor of the month.

As it happened, neither Alex nor Dave got direct help from their communities. Alex got lucky instead and gradually lost interest in the attention her students gave her as she started to integrate more with her colleagues, and dances then became a time to socialize with them and not with students. As she affiliated more with colleagues, her students saw her more as an adult than as one of them and they went searching for another teacher to anoint.

But Dave didn't fare so well. He became less interested in his teaching as his students became less interested in him, and he basically petered out and felt bitter and unsupported at the end of his career. During his last few years of teaching, Dave simply divested himself. He went through the motions but his spark as a teacher was gone. His students weren't harmed by his behavior, but they weren't helped either, and the school lost the efforts of a talented teacher long before he retired.

WHEN ADULTS LOOK TO TEENS TO GET THEIR NEEDS MET

Looking to students for affirmation, like Alex and Dave did, is an occupational hazard of working in the teenage world. The thrill of being included by teens can be positively intoxicating and, if left unchecked, can wreak havoc.

I don't know one teacher who doesn't want to be liked by students, so I believe all of us are at risk in this regard. The popularity that plays such an important role among students often spills over into the adult community, and Alex and Dave, for example, were highly susceptible to its allure. Fortunately, no damage was done to students in either scenario, despite the blurring of boundaries, particularly in Alex's case. (Although you could argue that Dave's students were hurt because he became less invested in his work as he approached retirement.) Sometimes, however, we aren't so lucky and the allure of the situation takes over, and when this happens both student and teacher alike may suffer considerable harm.

The Case of Peter

Peter was not a popular teacher in the conventional sense. He did his job well, though, and he was liked by his students. He stayed below the radar screen, for the most part, until he met Jill, a senior in his English seminar. Jill was drawn to Peter's sense of humor and intellectual prowess and Peter felt flattered. Jill wrote entries to him in her class journal and Peter often wrote lengthy comments in response.

Peter began to look forward to Jill's notes and felt excited when her writing became more personal and confessional. Jill wrote of her hopes and fears about college, her ambivalence about her boyfriend, and finally about her growing attachment to Peter. Peter responded in kind and confessed that he, too, was growing attached.

Peter knew his growing feelings for Jill were not appropriate but he also didn't want to stop the flow of the attention he was getting. He rationalized his behavior by reasoning that he didn't want to hurt Jill or make her feel awkward by pulling away. He convinced himself that his flirtation was harmless and that any change in his behavior would be ill advised.

Then Jill's mother found Jill's journal, and Peter was out of a job.

I offer the example of Peter as a cautionary tale. Peter was not a pedophile, he did not have a pattern of preying on his female students, and he felt deeply sorry for his behavior. He was an ordinary teacher whose vulnerabilities were no greater than any other adult's. He got seduced not by Jill, per se, but by the allure of the attention and affirmation he received from her.

For the record, I believe it is always the adult's responsibility to contain circumstances like this. Jill could have come to class naked and still it would have been Peter's responsibility to contain the situation. To suggest a child can seduce a teacher is to assign responsibility for the situation to the child, which is never appropriate. Teachers can be seduced, of course, but it is by our own vulnerabilities that we are seduced, not by our actual students. All of us have weaknesses and needs that may emerge in the course of our work, and sometimes we don't even know they're there. Peter didn't know he had them and this is why it's so important for us to think about these things—not because we will do exactly what Peter did, but because we will do something.

Peter was trying to get legitimate needs met in illegitimate ways. He was lonely. He and his students were vulnerable because he wasn't getting his emotional needs met elsewhere, and this increased his susceptibility to crossing over the line. Peter's loneliness wasn't caused by teaching but it was exacerbated by it, and given the nature of his transgression no other teacher could have seen it coming. He wasn't like Alex, dancing in public for everyone to see. When we start feeling lonely or isolated in our work in the teenage world, as Peter did, we should talk to someone about it immediately. Had Peter known to do this he could have saved himself, his students, and his school a lot of heartache.

THEY DON'T REALLY CARE ABOUT YOU

The heightened emotionality and drama of the teenage world throws adults off balance and sometimes it gets us into trouble. Peter learned this lesson the hard way, and fortunately his behavior didn't transgress a physical boundary. Peter was lucky that Jill's mother intervened when she did otherwise the scenario might have become very dangerous.

Sadly, Peter could have avoided this trouble if he'd understood the most essential creed of the teenage world: They really don't care about you.

It is compelling to think our students care about us as people but the truth is, they don't. Teachers always fight me on this point. They offer countless examples of students asking them questions about their personal lives, etc., as proof that their students are interested in them as people. This is how I respond: The next time a student asks you something about yourself, assuming that it is not too personal or provocative, respond truthfully. You might even throw in an inane tidbit or two about your life. Then get out your stopwatch, start the timer, and see how long it takes for your student's eyes to glaze over as you respond.

The fact is, students are interested in us to the extent in which we are interested in them. They lose interest in us quickly when our interest shifts to ourselves, as you will witness if you conduct this experiment. This is due, in part, to the natural self-absorption of the average teen but also to the fact that it's not their job to be interested in us. We don't really exist for them as people beyond the roles we play in their lives, and that's how it should be.

Peter might have responded differently to Jill if someone had explained this to him. (Admittedly, there are some teachers for whom this caution isn't sufficient. When teachers transgress boundaries constantly and when those transgressions are egregious, that's about the teacher, not the phenomenon of adolescence. I will return to this point in chapter 6.)

Alex, Dave, and Peter all got affected by the feverish attraction of adolescence because they thought the situation was about them and not their students. Alex wanted to believe she was as cool as her students thought she was. She succumbed to the conceit that she was special because she was more hip and fun than other teachers. Dave wanted to believe he was the best teacher in the school. He believed his popularity emanated from him and not from his students. Peter wanted to feel special, important, and attractive. He thought his relationship with Jill was appropriate and reciprocal.

THE MYTH OF RECIPROCITY

If we follow the point about our students' disinterest in us to its logical conclusion, we are left with the realization that there is no reciprocity in our relationships with students, and that reciprocity between students and teachers is a myth. I sometimes get pushback on this point from adults, so let me explain.

Some school communities and teaching philosophies deemphasize the power differential between teacher and student. This is fine; there's nothing categorically wrong with this. But deemphasizing and denying are different things. When the inherent differences between the roles of adult and student are denied, everyone is affected and the adolescent perspective can take over.

Adults are in charge in schools. Adults have the power to evaluate and discipline students and these two responsibilities create an inevitable and important power differential. Alex and Peter especially would have done well to remember this during their respective interactions with students. They could have used this as an antidote to resist the allure of their respective situations.

THE GOOD NEWS:
ADOLESCENCE ISN'T DEADLY (USUALLY)

We all have to understand how we respond to the phenomenon of adolescence because we all get affected by it, and our teenage students, in one way or another. Our situation may look different than Alex's or Dave's or Peter's but that's no reason to feel complacent. The good news, however, is that the effects of adolescence aren't deadly, usually. Rarely does a teacher succumb completely to the infection.

So, we can be infected through our working in the teenage world and the prognosis can be good, but only if we recognize what's going on and deal with the fever when it hits. The prognosis is not so good if we ignore what's going on and allow our fever to increase, like Peter did.

WHEN SCHOOLS GET AFFECTED BY ADOLESCENCE

The phenomenon of adolescence affects school communities as readily as it does individual teachers. An affected community can be hard to recognize from within because the resulting atmosphere can seem normal if the effect is widespread. Therefore, all of us in the adult community should be on the lookout for the following telltale signs of school-wide infection.

First, chances are good that adolescence has a grip on the community when adults gossip about other adults and/or students, for example, when teachers use their lunch hour to discuss the social lives of students. Also, when communication among adults is unclear, goes underground, or is mostly negative, then school communities are at risk of behaving just like their teenage students.

Second, when the popularity of teachers becomes a valuable currency, you've got trouble. Some teachers will always be better liked than others; this is inevitable. But when cults of personality are left unchecked, or when cult-like devotion to teachers is considered par for the course, that's a sure sign that the standards of adolescence and not adulthood predominate within the school culture.

Third, when there is ongoing difficulty between faculty and administration, an adolescent attitude can be the cause. An "us vs. them" mentality is very telling, as is an atmosphere where teachers routinely and/or openly side with students without first trying to understand the administrative position. Inevitably, when adults don't support each other there's a problem. This aspect of adolescent behavior is most potent when adults gossip with students about other teachers, administrators, or school policies.

Fourth, when clear expectations for adult behavior are not established and reinforced, the community is vulnerable. When adults do not like or respect one another or the administration, or when they see their connections to each other as unimportant, risk of starting to behave just like teenagers is high.

Each school is different and therefore the phenomenon of adolescence will play out differently within every community, just as it does with individuals. But some things remain constant about infection and are clear indicators that the adolescent mindset has taken over: a feeling of chaos, a high degree of reactivity or impulsivity, poor judgment, and inconsistent decision-making within the adult population. Evidence of any of these things points to infection and should be addressed immediately to provide containment. (See chapter 6 for a more detailed discussion of community-wide responses to adolescence.)

THE EVEN BETTER NEWS

Working in the hot zone is challenging and it takes patience but, as all teachers know, challenge and patience are essential for growth and mastery. Understanding ourselves is the mandate of the parallel curriculum, and I believe this is a gift. Most professionals can survive without ever having to explore themselves. Adults who work in the teenage world cannot afford this luxury. It might seem like an inconvenience to understand ourselves but we should never confuse convenience with satisfaction. The satisfaction we get from recognizing our vulnerabilities and fostering our strengths is the best course of treatment for working in the teenage world, and the personal payoffs are huge, a point I will return to in the next chapter.

When we understand how teenagers and their adolescent brains affect us in our work we can better understand ourselves, and the knowledge we gain in the process pays incalculable dividends in our work in the teenage world. It also helps us survive when we get caught in the teenage maelstrom.

EXERCISES AND REFLECTIONS

1. What were some of your biggest challenges as a middle and high school student? (Academics? Social life? Athletics? Extracurricular activities?) In what areas of your life did you feel confident or unconfident?

2. Consider a challenge you faced or one area in which you felt unconfident as a teenager and consider how this might affect your current work with students. Consider, also, how your experiences of confidence might affect your work. (For example, if you were very studious as a teen, you might favor such students.)

3. Why did you become a teacher? What expectations did you have about the profession? Which expectations have been met and which haven't? How satisfied are you with your work?

4. What kinds of teachers did you have as a teenager? Did you have any role models from your past that inform your current work with teenagers?

5. Why do you choose to work with adolescents? What experience did you have working with teens prior to becoming a teacher? How much training did you receive in adolescent development, group dynamics, or classroom management before you started working in the teenage world? What preparation did you receive

for dealing with the phenomenon of adolescence, and how well does it serve you?

6. Consider a time when you felt affected by your students. This might include situations in which you were swept up in their emotions or drama, or felt reactive in a heated situation. What did you do in the situation? Did you discuss the situation with a colleague or seek support or guidance?

7. When have you transgressed a boundary with a student? Transgression takes various forms, some of which were discussed throughout this chapter. A transgression might take the following forms: treating students differently or specially; sharing unnecessary or personal information with students; or ignoring troubling behavior. (This may not seem like a boundary transgression but it is. When teachers ignore student behavior it means students are allowed to continue with their boundary transgressions.) What happened when you transgressed the boundary? How did your student react? How did other adults in your school community react? What would you do differently in the future to prevent the transgression?

8. Consider a situation in which a colleague got caught up in the teenage firestorm. What happened? Why do you think they got affected as they did? How was the situation handled? What would you have done in this situation?

9. If Alex, Dave, or Peter were your colleagues and came to you for advice, how would you respond to their situations? How do you think you would respond if you were in their shoes?

CHAPTER SUMMARY

Adults who work in the teenage world exist in the hot zone of the phenomenon of adolescence and invariably it affects them. This means teenagers affect adults and adult behavior in schools, as the case studies in this chapter suggest. Adults are vulnerable to the behavior of teenagers for various reasons, such as when they look to get their own needs met by the teenagers they work with. Adults can use their relationship with teens to better understand themselves, which in turn helps them be more effective in their work in the teenage world.

3

THE SEVEN GROWN-UP SKILLS

Adults who work in the teenage world must practice *seven grown-up skills* to deal effectively with the phenomenon of adolescence. When we practice these skills our behavior is grown-up and when we don't practice them our behavior is grown-older. Throughout the chapter I explore the distinctions between grown-up and grown-older behavior and suggest that we all should practice the seven grown-up skills if we want to have healthy relationships with our students.

PROTECTING OURSELVES FROM THE PHENOMENON OF ADOLESCENCE

Those of us who work in the hot zone of the teenage world can protect ourselves from the affects of adolescence by practicing seven skills that serve to distinguish our behavior from that of our teenage students. When we practice the *seven grown-up skills*, as I call them, we behave differently than teenagers do. We behave like grown-ups. When we don't practice these skills we behave more like teenagers themselves. We behave like *grown-olders*, as I like to say.

The seven grown-up skills serve adults and our teenage students because these skills help us manage the developing teenage brain. Without these skills, we are at the mercy of the teenage experience, which is not where we want to be, believe me.

The seven grown-up skills are:

1. Self-Awareness
2. Self-Control/Self-Mastery
3. Good Judgment
4. The Ability to Deal with Conflict
5. Self-Transcendence, or the Ability to Get Over Yourself
6. The Ability to Maintain Boundaries
7. The Capacity for Life-Long Learning

The seven grown-up skills increase our ability to deal effectively with our teenage students, and when we practice them we bounce back quicker from mistakes, are better at our work, and are much happier at our jobs than when we don't.

WHAT IS A GROWN-UP?

Let's pause for a moment to ask an important question: What is a grown-up, anyway?[1] Well, *grown-up* is a hard term to define. Grown-ups are many things, really, and no two grown-ups look alike. Therefore I will begin by considering what a grown-up *is not*.

WHAT A GROWN-UP IS NOT

It's Not About Age

First, being grown-up is not about age. Age has something to do with it, of course, as our understanding of brain development suggests. Teenagers, for example, behave like grown-ups at times but that doesn't mean that they are grown-up, regardless of how mature they seem. And while teenagers sometimes act like grown-ups, adults sometimes act like teens, so age is no guarantee of being grown-up.

It's Not a Destination

Second, being grown-up is not the end-point of a developmental phase, it's a process that continues throughout adulthood. Psychological maturity does not occur in a linear fashion, nor does it proceed along a clear trajectory. It unfolds differently for each of us, and there are ups and downs along the way.

It's Not Inevitable

Third, being grown-up is not inevitable. We have a choice about whether we practice grown-up skills. Not everyone chooses to grow up. Some folks just grow older.

BEING GROWN-UP IS A SKILL

Given this issue of intention, it is helpful to think of being grown-up as a skill, or set of skills, that adults acquire through understanding, practice, and patience. Growing up can be understood, then, as a process of acquiring skills, and grown-up as the state of being in which adults exhibit these skills, behaviors, and attitudes. According to this schema, the world isn't divided between adults who have reached a state of psychological maturity and those who have not, but rather between adults who practice grown-up skills regularly and those who don't. I think this is a more generous distinction because it implies we can all act like grown-ups *if we want to*, which is true, for the most part. It also keeps us accountable in our work with teenagers because if being grown-up is about intention, then there's no excuse for us not to practice grown-up skills.

WHY GROWN-UP SKILLS MATTER

Grown-up skills distinguish adults from adolescents in the teenage world, and therefore the practice of grown-up skills is critical to our success in our work with teenagers, simply critical. If we didn't need to be different from our students, then older kids could just teach younger kids, or smarter kids could teach less smart kids—students wouldn't need adults at all. But we know this wouldn't work. Why? Because teenagers need something more from us than just our content knowledge. Teenagers need us to not only *know* more than they do, they need us to *be* more than they are, and this is where the seven grown-up skills come into play. These skills separate the adult wheat from the adolescent chaff, so to speak, and when we practice and master these skills we ensure that our world and the teenage world remain healthy and distinct.

THE SEVEN GROWN-UP SKILLS

The following are explanations of each of the seven grown-up skills, along with case studies of each skill being practiced, or not being practiced, as the case may be. Please note that the best way to make use of these concepts is to try them on for size—see how they apply to your own experience. The purpose of thinking about these skills is to improve our work with students, and hopefully to understand ourselves better. I therefore suggest you take time to reflect upon your own strengths and challenges in relation to each skill, and consider how each skill comes into play in your work in the teenage world.

Rest assured, we *all* face challenges with every skill at some point during our careers. No one is perfect, and no one practices the grown-up skills perfectly everyday. But we all must think about our behavior with our students, and I believe the seven grown-up skills help us to clarify our responsibilities in this important aspect of our work with teenagers.

Skill 1: Self-Awareness

The first grown-up skill is self-awareness. When we practice the skill of self-awareness we step back and take an objective look at ourselves. This capacity for reflection is the foundation of true psychological maturity. Without this skill, we can't receive or understand feedback or criticism, or make use of it. The skill of self-awareness leads to psychological perspective and, by extension, to insight. Without it, we can't see beyond our own psychological trees, and this is a real liability for those of us who work with teenagers.

The following are some questions we can ask ourselves to encourage self-exploration and guide us to increased self-awareness:

1. How do we come across to others? How closely does our self-perception match the perception others have of us?
2. What are our positive and negative traits? How do we accept feedback on these traits, especially the ones we don't like?
3. Do we apply the same standards to ourselves as to others? Do we let ourselves off the hook for behavior we expect others to exhibit? Conversely, do we let others off the hook and demand more of ourselves than is reasonable?

4. What drives our behavior? What are our primary motivations, especially in regards to our work?
5. What are our core values and beliefs?
6. How do we understand our internal dialogue, or the conversation we have with ourselves in our head? What are some of the repeating narratives we tell ourselves, and are these narratives useful?
7. Can we identify when we are having strong feelings, and can we identify what these feelings are?

The answers to these questions can help us understand who we are, why we do what we do, and what really matters to us. The answers can also help us in our work with teenagers. Remember, teenagers don't know who they are yet; they're just beginning to ask themselves these questions. The more facility we have with asking these questions the more we can help teens in their own process of self-discovery, and this will come in handy when they get caught up in their adolescent chaos, as well as when this chaos affects us.

The Case of Heather

Heather, an experienced fine arts teacher, was like many of us in that she didn't know she should ask herself these questions, especially the ones about feedback and how she came across to others. She frequently made ill-advised comments to students that inevitably worked their way back to her supervisor, and whenever she was asked to explain her comments or her motivation for making them, she was unable to do so. Heather did not practice the skill of self-awareness and subsequently she didn't understand herself or her behavior very well.

For example, once, in her sincere desire to inquire about a student's health, Heather asked her student publicly about her treatment for anorexia. Her student felt humiliated by Heather's inquiry, and when she hesitated to respond to Heather's request for information, Heather continued along the same lines of questioning. Heather not only didn't understand what she was doing, she also didn't understand how her behavior affected her student, and naturally this came to her supervisor's attention.

Because she was bright, Heather could recall the specifics of what she had said, but because she did not practice the skill of self-awareness, she was unable to understand her motivation for making her comments or why someone else might perceive her comments differently than she did. Heather's interest in her student's health was justified but her method of inquiry indicated that she lacked a recognition of the sensitivity of the situation.

Over time, Heather was not able to make use of the feedback she received from her supervisor and both of them became frustrated, but for different reasons. Heather, for her part, made sure to never make the same comment twice, but because she never understood why these comments were inappropriate, she continued to make mistakes, saying the wrong thing at the wrong time. Her supervisor, on the other hand, felt an increasing disturbance at Heather's lack of self-awareness in the face of repeated incidents and conversations. Despite her best efforts, one year Heather's contract was not renewed and, sadly, she didn't see it coming. Without the ability to see herself as others saw her, Heather was unable to understand what had happened.

Heather's situation illustrates an important point about this grown-up skill, and perhaps about all of them. Practicing grown-up skills is not correlated with intelligence, for the most part. Ironically, intelligence can hinder the practice of grown-up skills because smart people can often think themselves right out of their problems (only to have them resurface later, of course). This is what happened with Heather. She was bright and well-educated but she was unaware of her own psychological process.

Like Heather, all of us have our blindspots when it comes to understanding ourselves. We may have clear vision in one area only to be clouded in another, which is why we need trusted colleagues and mentors to help us see ourselves objectively. This process can sting, but if we start with the assumption that none of us is perfect, then hopefully we can accept the need to regularly scrutinize ourselves. We always have something more to learn about ourselves—we never conquer this mountain—so we should embrace this process if we can.

Perhaps Heather didn't embrace this process because she feared she would learn something horrible about herself. Or maybe she didn't want to appear like she didn't have all the answers. Many of us have these fears, but we must resist them. Had Heather looked at herself she would have discovered that her behavior was neither unethical nor unforgivable, it was just consistent. Heather was no different than the rest of us, specifics aside. We all have our lessons to learn, and we can't have all the answers. We're just supposed to commit to the process of self-discovery and keep showing up.

In the end, self-awareness is an essential skill for adults working with teenagers to have because, like all of the other grown-up skills, it is precisely what teenagers *don't* have. Adolescents are just beginning to develop self-awareness, and if we don't practice it ourselves, we can't help our students develop this critical skill. (More on how to cultivate self-awareness in chapter 7.)

Skill 2: Self-Control/Self-Mastery

The second grown-up skill is self-control/self-mastery. When we practice self-control we do something that teenagers can't when it comes to their impulses: We can keep a lid on our id. When we practice self-control we are able to monitor our thoughts, feelings, and desires and not act upon them in a knee-jerk manner. When we practice the more advanced skill of self-mastery, we are able to direct our energy and attention with purpose and intention. The skill of self-control comes first and, when practiced over time, the skill of self-mastery follows.

Self-control is an essential skill for us to practice because our relationships with teenagers are most challenging when teenage impulses are out of control. Imagine, for a moment, an unsupervised middle school cafeteria at lunch time. The adolescent fever can spread quickly if it isn't contained, and when we don't practice self-control we just add to the epidemic. When we don't have the skill to control our own impulses, there's little hope we can help teenagers rein themselves in.[2]

The Case of Rachelle

Rachelle sometimes had challenges in this regard. Rachelle was a member of the math department and had a quick temper; like many of us, when she was tired, she felt even less in control. Rachelle's feelings occasionally got the better of her and, when they did, she was at their mercy.

Rachelle came from a family where the free expression of feelings was encouraged. The behavior of some of her out-of-control teenage students felt very familiar to her, and after a day in their midst she sometimes had trouble controlling herself. Unfortunately for Rachelle, all-school assemblies were sometimes scheduled for the end of the day, by which time she felt exhausted and depleted.

During a heated debate at one assembly, and after a long day in the classroom, Rachelle challenged the person running the meeting. In trying to make her point, she raised her voice and expressed opinions that normally she would have kept to herself. Basically, she lost it, and in the moment she wasn't able to control herself. Just like many of her teenage students, Rachelle felt relieved after blowing off steam, but only momentarily. She quickly realized what she had done and felt ashamed and regretful about her behavior.

While Rachelle didn't practice self-control during the assembly, she did practice self-awareness afterward, and as a result she went straight to her principal's office after the assembly to apologize for her behavior. She also sent her colleagues an email of apology and arranged to address the student body to express her regrets. Rachelle took what could have been a volatile situation and brought it under control, and in so doing practiced the self-control she hadn't displayed in her initial moment of vulnerability.

As I tell my teenage students, we all make mistakes; it's how we deal with our mistakes that's important. Like Rachelle, we need to mop up our mess as quickly as possible. Rachelle's case provides a wonderful example of how we should take responsibility for our missteps. Because Rachelle took account of her actions, the rest of the community was able to forgive and forget, although she never did. Rachelle remembered the incident for a long time afterward, and the memory helped her manage her feelings better as time passed. This is the practice of self-mastery, and a sincere and well-placed apology can go a long way to righting the wrongs we commit when we lapse in our self-control.

The Case of Mark

Mark's lack of self-control looked different than Rachelle's. For one thing, Mark never lost his temper the way Rachelle did, in part because he didn't really have a temper to lose. Instead, Mark didn't practice self-control when it came to his speech, which posed as big a challenge.

Mark was well-known among students for his casual comments, particularly when it came to his personal life. Mark let slip details about his love life, his problems with friends, his thoughts about his colleagues. Mark made the classic mistake of thinking that his comments indicated that he was mature and relatable, a mistake many of us make. His students loved Mark's comments because they invariably got him off the task of teaching. His students learned that a well-placed question could postpone the hard work of learning for long stretches at a time. And this is what happened on occasion. Mark made off-the-cuff comments, his students asked irrelevant questions, and another class got mired in the muck because he didn't understand the need to practice self-control.

As Mark's situation illustrates, when we don't practice the skill of self-control we are ineffective in our work, in part because our behavior matches our students'. Mark's students responded to his episodes of lack of self-control with lapses of their own, and then all bets were off. Soon, everything was out of control. Good classroom management begins with the skill of self-control, and Mark didn't practice it consistently. Without it, good teaching doesn't occur consistently either.

Cases like Mark's don't usually come under the scrutiny of the entire community, as Rachelle's did. Mark's behavior was mostly invisible to the adult community, despite the fact that students talked about his conduct to their other teachers on occasion. But what were Mark's colleagues supposed to do about the situation? His transgressions really couldn't be verified, and teenagers say things about teachers all the time, don't they?

I will explore the issue of how adults can support one another in chapter 5, but for now let me say that Mark needed lots of support from his community, including receiving clear behavioral guidelines and having trusted colleagues and administrators with whom he could discuss his work. All of us need a place to turn where we can talk about our challenges, because we all encounter them. Even if we don't chat about our personal lives with students like Mark did, we do something; we have some area in which we feel a lack of control, and this becomes a weak spot in our work. Mark needed someone to advise him on the practice of self-control and on his judgment calls when it came to his speech.

Skill 3: Good Judgment

The third grown-up skill is good judgment. Practicing good judgment is a critical part of our responsibility in the teenage world. Teenagers are often hard-pressed to practice good judgment themselves because their brains are still developing. They therefore need us to practice this skill when they can't, and to challenge their faulty teenage decision-making. In the end, teenagers need to be surrounded by adults who can protect them from themselves when necessary, and this is where our good judgment comes into play.

The Case of Bill

Bill, a seasoned science teacher, couldn't protect his students from their own poor judgment because he didn't have good judgment of his own. Bill's judgment, not to mention his skills of self-control and self-awareness, was woefully underdeveloped, and this caused him to make a big mess in the teenage world.

Bill routinely found himself attracted to his female students, particularly the physically and intellectually precocious girls in his junior classes. Adults in the teenage world must halt such attractions immediately, before they go anywhere. Bill didn't. One year his crush was reciprocated by Laura, a beautiful and brilliant sixteen-year-old, and Bill didn't exert good judgment in the relationship, let alone good impulse control.

Bill worked at a boarding school and had access to students around the clock, so he could easily arrange meetings with Laura. This proximity fueled his desire, and during one late-night extra-help session, Bill initiated a sexual relationship with Laura. Bill's connection to Laura lasted for more than a year, until after her graduation, and the only person who knew about it was Bill's wife Jessica, a fellow teacher. Her collusion in the situation illustrates another form of poor judgment—covering up for a colleague—one that may be easier to fall prey to than Bill's. Jessica remained the only other person to know about Bill and Laura's relationship until Laura spilled the beans years later, by which point Bill was dead.

Had Bill's behavior been discovered while it was occurring, he should have been confronted immediately and his behavior should have been reported to the appropriate authorities. The law is very clear about sexual relationships between adults and minors; they're not allowed under any circumstances,[3] and schools should respond swiftly and decisively when they occur. But if we consider Bill's attraction to his student, apart from his poor judgment about acting upon it, we enter into a territory many of us who work with teenagers occupy.

Adults sometimes become attracted to students. It happens. As I stated earlier, though, we must *never* act on this attraction. But this doesn't mean we should ignore what's happening. When we find ourselves sexually attracted to a student, we must deal with it immediately, which usually involves talking about it to a trusted and disinterested third party (and by disinterested I mean someone who has the presence of mind not to encourage our attraction). Dealing with our attraction in this way displays very good judgment on our part, and should go a long way to diffusing the situation.

Only a small number of us exercise poor judgment and lack of self-control to the degree Bill did. But many, like Bill's wife Jessica, have difficulty in the face of the poor judgment of others. Obviously Jessica had her own reasons for keeping quiet about Bill's behavior, reasons that superseded her role as a fellow teacher, but many teachers get caught in the grip of someone else's grown-older behavior and exercise poor judgment as a result. This was the case for Dawn.

The Case of Dawn

Dawn was a novice history teacher who was eager to do well. She was assigned to travel in a van during a class field trip with Brent, her mentor and fellow history teacher, and she was horrified to note that Brent sped, changed lanes erratically, and encouraged his students to spiral out of control throughout the drive.

Dawn made a passing comment to Brent about this, only to have him shrug off her concerns. Brent added something to the effect that his behavior with students had come under the scrutiny of their department chair and that he was on a short leash. Brent added that he was glad Dawn had joined the department because she seemed so cool and understanding.

Dawn was unsure how to deal with the situation. She knew Brent's behavior was unacceptable but she worried about his reaction if she expressed her concerns to their department chair. If Brent truly was on a short leash, then Dawn feared this additional information would get him into serious trouble. In addition, Brent, as her mentor, was helping

Dawn navigate her first teaching job and he was being very helpful. So she kept her concerns to herself.

As soon as we feel isolated as professionals, as Dawn did, this is a sign we need help. Dawn needed help to sort through what was happening with Brent, and her students needed protection from Brent's unsafe behavior. Dawn knew someone needed to speak to Brent, but she didn't feel it was her responsibility. That's understandable, and possibly accurate, but it was her responsibility to talk to someone who could intervene in the situation. Dawn had enough good judgment to recognize that students were unsafe in Brent's care, and she needed to act on this impulse, not on her fear of getting Brent into trouble. Nobody could help Dawn until she sought help for herself. She needed a trusted supervisor to help her sort through her feelings and deal with Brent's poor judgment.

Again, when we feel isolated, this is a sign we need help, and asking for help is the best practice of good judgment there is.

Skill 4: Ability to Deal with Conflict

The fourth grown-up skill is the ability to deal productively with conflict. Dawn's poor judgment arose from her desire to avoid conflict, something very common among teachers, in my experience. Teachers are the good guys, we want to be liked by students and each other (which is not a bad thing), and conflict among colleagues is often regarded as unacceptable. But adults disagree all the time, and when we practice this grown-up skill we learn how to manage conflict productively. This doesn't mean we have to like conflict, but we should learn how to deal with it. More schools stagnate due to lack of open and mature disagreement than any other reason, and when we don't practice the skill of dealing with conflict among ourselves, our students are left to navigate their conflicting worlds on their own.

Every school wants to create a community in which people get along. This is admirable, but we can get along even better when we know how to confront our issues productively, and this is what this skill aims to promote. Had Dawn been able to talk to Brent directly, or to someone else in a position to mediate the situation, both she and Brent would have been better for it. True, there may have been some discomfort or even hurt feelings along the way, but Dawn would have been able to tell her truth, help a colleague who needed help, and Brent could have received invaluable feedback about his performance. Not all easy, but all good.

The Case of Joanne

Joanne, like many of us, did not like conflict, with students or with colleagues. Joanne worked for decades at a school that didn't like conflict either, and therefore Joanne dealt with conflict only sporadically because the school's practices were in line with her own. Joanne felt a lot of conflict internally, though—about her teaching, her standing among her colleagues, her intelligence—in part because she'd never learned to accept and master her own feelings, so when conflict arose at work, which it invariably did, Joanne felt ill-equipped to deal with it.

One day Joanne was present during a heated discussion about a disciplinary issue that involved some of her students. Joanne had strong feelings about the subject: She believed the students should be punished for their behavior, although, given her difficulty with conflict, she didn't want to be the one to punish them. She didn't want to make her students feel any discomfort, and she definitely didn't want to be the bad guy or risk feeling any discomfort herself. Joanne's discomfort with conflict was so extreme that when asked her opinion about possible consequences for the students, she lied in an effort to avoid disagreement. And not only did she lie, she went out of her way to agree with an opinion she didn't support.

Had it ended there, it might not have mattered much, except to Joanne's conscience. But Joanne was so exercised at dealing with conflict in her own way that after the meeting she went straight to a colleague and started to vent. In discussing the situation as they did, Joanne and her colleague inadvertently set in motion a process that threatened to undermine their colleagues and the outcome of the disciplinary process. As often happens in situations like this, frustration and dissention spread around the community, which caused the situation to escalate. Not surprisingly, this caused Joanne's hope of avoiding conflict to backfire, and the thing she feared most was at her doorstep when the principal got involved.

In an effort to practice dealing with conflict, Joanne might have examined her own thoughts and feelings before reporting them to someone else, and after sorting them through, she might have spoken to someone involved with the situation about her concerns. It's not necessary that we be experts in our practice, just that we stay engaged in the process of communication and not subvert it, like Joanne unintentionally did.

We owe it to ourselves and to the community to share our opinion in important situations, and Joanne was denying the community important data by withholding her opinion. Had she understood the situation from this perspective she may have been more willing to participate directly, comfortable or not. Sadly, Joanne didn't recognize that she was an essential part of the group's functioning, and that her opinion would have strengthened the process, rather than threatened it.

Whereas dealing with conflict is an essential skill to master, comfort with conflict doesn't necessarily mark the grown-up. Some adults embrace conflict in the same way teenagers do, and within the teenage world such behavior often gets rewarded by students and provides us with a disincentive to exercise this skill. To this end, inciting or rejoicing in conflict is just as destructive as avoiding it. When we practice this grown-up skill we can tolerate conflict *and* resolve it, which is invaluable for our students.

Finally, and perhaps most importantly, it's essential for us to be able to deal with conflict because teenagers, without fail, will go out of their way to create conflict with us—it's part of their parallel curriculum—and therefore we must be able to tolerate the discomfort we feel when this happens. If we don't or can't deal with conflict, then we will have a hard time giving our students what they need, which sometimes is simply the presence of an adult who can tolerate their chaos without succumbing to it. We must be able to make sense of conflict with and among teenagers, put clear guidelines in place about our expectations for their behavior, and deal with situations when they get out of hand.

Skill 5: Self-Transcendence, or the Ability to Get Over Yourself

The fifth grown-up skill is self-transcendence, or the ability to just get over ourselves. Joanne had trouble doing this. She couldn't see beyond her own conflicted feelings to understand how her behavior affected her colleagues or students. When we practice the skill of self-transcendence we have the capacity to do this, and we help everyone within the community when we do.

Someone once said, "I may not mean much to you but *I'm* all *I* think about." This statement captures what most of us are thinking most of the time, and there's nothing wrong with it. But those of us who work with teenagers must force ourselves beyond this position, at least when we're at work. We must transcend ourselves in order to be of service to others. We must put the needs of others first.

There are two ways that adults who work in schools demonstrate the skill of self-transcendence. The first is to understand the importance of cooperation and collaboration. When we practice this skill we see ourselves as part of a larger system that functions to support the growth of students. The second is to understand that we can't take everything personally. When we practice this skill we have the capacity to determine when something is about us and when it's not.

The Case of Frank

Frank, a committed physics teacher, had difficulty seeing himself as part of the school community. He had his doctorate and taught at the university level before teaching in high schools. He liked the autonomy of the classroom, which is what drew him to teaching in the first place, and he appreciated his bright and eager students. But Frank wanted to be left alone at work. He was what I call a rogue teacher.

Frank didn't participate in faculty meetings, avoided all non-compulsory school events, and didn't want to serve as an advisor to students. He couldn't be swayed in his position despite the difficulties this created for his colleagues, who had to pick up his slack from time to time. Luckily for Frank, he was a competent instructor, but his lack of interest and engagement beyond the classroom was problematic and his colleagues thought he was selfish.

Frank failed to recognize that he existed in a community, and that his role as a teacher of adolescents meant he had to get over his desire to go it alone. Frank enjoyed instructing his students and he loved his subject matter, but he thought this was enough. He didn't understand that his refusal to engage with his colleagues meant he was considering his needs exclusively, often at the expense of the needs of others. In the end, no one else mattered to Frank. He just couldn't get over himself.

Frank's attitude was fueled by what he considered to be the selfishness of his students. Even though he enjoyed instructing them, he saw them for what they were: self-absorbed adolescents. His proximity to students all day long did nothing to help his own self-absorption, a risk we all face in our work. Frank didn't appreciate that what was for them an appropriate developmental phase was for him an indication of developmental arrest.

Frank's attitude was apparent to everyone in the community, so in a sense the entire community failed him when they didn't give him feedback about his behavior. Frank made it clear that he didn't want to interact with his colleagues, and so his colleagues treated him in kind, thus missing an opportunity to help him integrate into their fold. While ultimately it was Frank's responsibility to connect with others, the community had a responsibility to connect to him too, and if his colleagues and supervisors meant business, then they needed to give Frank some guidance. This didn't happen, though, and Frank was permitted to remain a rogue.

Frank's situation is a difficult one because teachers often don't feel comfortable giving feedback to their colleagues. This raises the question of responsibility, and of who's responsible for intervening in such matters. Someone needed to help Frank. By the very nature of his challenge he wasn't going to be able to help himself, and yet this kind of problem can be quite vexing for teachers in schools. Teachers aren't usually each others keepers, and yet in some cases we must be. Is Frank's such a case? It depends on the community, and all of us need to engage with our communities to figure this out.

The Case of Anna

Frank's inability to acknowledge his connection to his surroundings stood in stark contrast to Anna's. Anna, an experienced math teacher, was involved with everything at school. She went out of her way to know what was going on with her students, and she encouraged her students to confide in her. Anna loved her students and, as a measure of that love, she took all of their adolescent dramas to heart.

One day Anna's class started to lose control. It was the first day of spring and her students were eager for class to end. Anna repeatedly asked them to settle down, but her requests turned into pleas as they got more boisterous. Anna wanted to support her students' enthusiasm but she also wanted them to stay on task. Anna felt overwhelmed by the situation, and also hurt. Wasn't she the teacher who always accommodated her students? Wasn't she the one who always was there for them? Didn't she deserve better treatment than this?

Finally, after some students starting throwing spitballs, Anna shouted, "How do you think this makes me feel?"

Anna's response to the situation revealed the challenges she faced, and her subsequent vulnerability when attempting to separate her own experience from that of her students. Anna took their behavior personally, and felt not only frustrated by the situation, as any teacher would, but also wounded. As Anna discovered, teenagers can sniff out vulnerability like hounds on the hunt. Her inability to transcend herself and to not take the situation personally was palpable to her students, which caused their behavior to escalate. Anna's response to the situation communicated to her students the paradoxical truth that she was simultaneously uncentered (and working her way to being unglued) and completely self-focused, at least in the moment.

Many of us have been in Anna's shoes, feeling frustrated and let down by our students' behavior. Anna's students weren't trying to wound her, though; and even if they had been, Anna could have helped her situation by seeing their behavior for what it was: adolescent acting out, which was not really about her. This can be hard to remember when we're trapped in the midst of teenage acting out, however, but the most effective thing Anna could have done was remain centered, not self-focused, which would have allowed her to take better control of the situation.

Teenagers are famous for their self-absorption, so those of us who work with them can't be. Whether self-absorption takes a classic form, like Frank's, or a more subtle form, like Anna's, we must remember our relative place in the teenage world. To this end, we must develop the skill of self-transcendence—or more precisely, of just getting over ourselves.

Skill 6: Ability to Maintain Boundaries

The sixth grown-up skill is the ability to maintain boundaries. Frank's boundaries with his students and colleagues were too rigid, while Anna's were too loose. So what's an adult in the teenage world to do? The crux of the boundary issue is this: Who's in charge, the adult or the teenager?

When we practice our grown-up skills in the teenage world, we know we are in charge and we don't lose sight of this fact even in the face of adversity. When we don't practice grown-up skills, or when we are confused by or uncomfortable setting boundaries, we lose sight of our role, which is what happened with Gianna.

The Case of Gianna

Gianna was an experienced middle school science teacher who loved her job and her students. She took pride in being cool and in having students confide in her. But Gianna thought she had to accommodate her students to maintain her popularity, and so when prompted she shared her own personal information during class, which is exactly what her students wanted her to do.

For example, during the 8th grade sexuality unit, Gianna disclosed her own sexual experiences and history to her students, and embellished the content of the curriculum with details from her own life. She believed what her students told her, that such revelations put them at ease and facilitated discussion about sensitive topics. Adding to her challenge, her students constantly asked her personal questions, and the truth was she didn't know how to say no to them.

In addition to not maintaining boundaries, Gianna didn't practice impulse control, but her reasons for disclosing personal information went beyond an inability to keep a lid on it. Gianna liked her students enormously, and like many of us she wanted their attention and affirmation. She wanted to relate to her students, and she mistook her practice of sharing personal information about herself as being relational and appropriate.

Gianna's situation is not uncommon: Many of us feel compelled to share personal information with students, and many students ask us to, making it hard sometimes for us to know where to draw the line. This was perhaps Gianna's biggest challenge, and it's one most of us face at some point in our work with teenagers. When our students are the people we deal with most, we can easily adopt their standards as our own. But when we realize these standards conflict with our school's, it's time to reexamine our behavior. When Gianna's department chair directed her to stop sharing personal information with students, Gianna did, although not surprisingly she continued to feel challenged by her students' questions.

In order to avoid Gianna's situation, we should be clear about what our community expects from us when it comes to our relationships with students, both inside and outside of the classroom. If we have questions or are uncertain about these standards, we should ask before we proceed. Many of us operate under the assumption that we should know all of this instinctively—that we shouldn't have to ask, or that asking indicates we aren't fully prepared or qualified—but this isn't the case. We can't possibly know everything all the time, and so we must ask for help, and then, when we have the information we need, we can establish and maintain appropriate boundaries with our students.

The Case of Rick

Rick had a much clearer sense of propriety than Gianna did, but he felt very uncomfortable with the amount of power he wielded in his role as teacher, and as a result he didn't know how to maintain boundaries with students. Rick believed passionately in equity and equality in the classroom, and by extension he believed that no real distinction should exist between teacher and student. No distinctions, no boundaries, or something along these lines.

This played itself out when Rick insisted that his students call him by his first name, which was not part of accepted practice within his school culture, and he allowed his students to run the show, for the most part. If students didn't want to follow his lesson plan, they didn't, and Rick justified this behavior on the grounds that his students ultimately knew what was best for them. Once, when he handed out a mid-term assignment that met with resistance, Rick backed down instantly. He acquiesced to his students' desires to not do the assigned work, and he measured his success as a teacher by the pleasure his students expressed with his behavior.

Rick did not understand that adolescents are not the best judges of their own needs. If they were, they wouldn't need teachers. Because he felt uncomfortable practicing grown-up skills, Rick abandoned his role as teacher and, as a result, abdicated responsibility for what happened in his classroom.

Rick got feedback about his behavior from his colleagues when it emerged that all his students received A's. When pressed to defend himself, Rick admitted that he had a hard time setting limits with his students and that he didn't know how to evaluate them properly. This was not easy for Rick to admit, but he had supportive colleagues who helped him examine his struggles and devise workable solutions, such as observing the class of a veteran teacher who had excellent classroom management skills. This proved helpful, as Rick was able to observe his colleague interact authentically with students and maintain good boundaries at the same time; and he was amazed to discover that his fellow teacher enjoyed enormous respect from his students, much more than he himself enjoyed.

The Case of Dan

Dan's challenge had more to do with his relationship with students outside the classroom than within. Dan, like Rick and Gianna, saw his students as peers, and as a result he wanted to cultivate their friendship. Dan often talked to his students about their personal lives (he didn't have much of one himself), and he found ways to be with his students in all kinds of activities. He joined them during lunch, at school events, and elsewhere whenever he could. He gave out his cell phone number and texted and emailed them frequently. He referred to them as his buddies and considered his relationship with them to be reciprocal.

Gianna, Rick, and Dan were all challenged when it came to maintaining boundaries, and they needed help to understand how to practice this important skill. They also needed to recognize that they were always on a learning curve, as we all are, and that receiving and incorporating support makes us stronger teachers and community members.

Skill 7: Life-Long Learning

The seventh and final grown-up skill is the ability to learn throughout life. *Life-long learning* for our purposes means learning about one's self, understanding one's personal psychology, and committing to this process in perpetuity. It also includes the capacity to explore relationships and pay attention to information about one's self that emerges within relationships, particularly relationships with teenagers.

This skill of perpetual self-discovery implies that we must be flexible, humble, and willing to accept change. It also implies that we accept responsibility for our actions. Life-long learning requires that we embrace our personal challenges and admit our mistakes, and that we be willing to adapt ourselves and our behavior whenever circumstances demand.

Finally, life-long learning is closely related to the first grown-up skill of self-awareness, and as such it brings us back full circle. Our need for life-long learning underscores the fact that mastering grown-up skills is a process that never ends.

Back to Dan

Let's return to Dan and consider how this process of insight and subsequent growth can occur. (Recall that Dan gave students his cell phone number and ate lunch with them often.) When approached by a colleague and questioned about how much time he spent with his students, Dan was able to admit after some initial defensiveness that he didn't have much of a social life outside of work. He also admitted that he felt intimidated by some of his colleagues (Dan was a relative novice and young teacher) and that hanging out with his students at lunch provided him with an excuse to avoid the faculty lounge. Dan, with the help of his colleague, was able to see that his method for dealing with his problems was neither appropriate nor effective. This insight didn't cause Dan to change overnight; however, it did set him on the right course.

Dan was able to make the changes he needed to make, like getting some interests and friends of his own and developing confidence around his colleagues, and thus avoid much bigger problems down the line. Dan was able to recognize his need for help, his students' need for him to maintain good boundaries, and his colleagues' need for him to join the ranks of the grown-up.

Working with teens sheds light on every vulnerability, insecurity, and unexamined complex we have. Just ask Dan. When we work with teens we get feedback about ourselves every day and, if we're wise, we use this feedback to improve ourselves. When we work in the teenage world, the grown-older's burden is the grown-up's opportunity for psychological growth and insight. Practicing the seven grown-up skills transforms us from good instructors into great educators because it ensures we understand our role in our relationships with teenagers.

We should keep this in mind when we feel tired or resistant or just don't want to make the effort.

NO ONE SAID THIS WOULD BE EASY

Each of the seven grown-up skills contributes something important to our healthy functioning in the teenage world, and each combines to help us take responsibility for ourselves and our actions in our work, but none of them is necessarily easy to implement, at least not initially. Nor does grown-up behavior come naturally; it has to be learned and practiced. In some ways, we have as much to learn in the teenage world as teenagers do, but unfortunately this part of the job doesn't come with an instruction manual. We have to commit to learning this stuff mostly on our own, or with the help of a good mentor, if we're lucky. But when we undertake thinking about our grown-up skill set and our practice of grown-up behavior, I can give you a money-back guarantee that our work as adults in the teenage world becomes more fulfilling and effective.

DOES EVERYONE HAVE TO GROW UP?

Does everyone have to practice grown-up skills? Well, yes, those of us who work in the teenage world have to. Of course, we all have a choice about whether to develop grown-up skills, and many of us make the choice not to develop them and not to grow up. For some adults this choice doesn't matter, at least not professionally. Who cares whether an accountant or a mail carrier or an attorney is grown-up? Some adults even are praised in our culture for not growing up, like some actors or professional athletes. These adults can do their jobs without concerning themselves with this stuff. But those of us who work with teenagers can't; we don't have this luxury. Those of us who work in the teenage world must practice grown-up skills if we want to be good at our jobs.

Here's the thing about developing grown-up skills, though: It's something everyone has to do for themselves. We can't force anyone to do it. And we have to *want* to do it ourselves; no one can compel us to develop psychologically against our wishes. Every person must determine for himself or herself how to navigate adulthood. That said, adults can support each other along the way, and that's one of the great benefits of working in a school community. While the work of growing up is our own, we needn't and shouldn't do it in isolation. Our colleagues should be there for us, as we should be there for our colleagues, helping one another to practice our grown-up skills.

So the real question follows, what's so great about growing up? Why should we want to do it?

GROWING UP IS WORTH IT

Working in the teenage world is incredibly challenging but I contend that practicing the seven grown-up skills makes it easier, more fulfilling, and hopefully more fun. When we practice these seven skills, we get much more pleasure out of our work because we don't get thrown off balance by the chaos of adolescence. We are able to roll with the punches, if you will, and in the process we do a much better job of doing our job.

Take any of the above-mentioned cases and imagine that the teacher in question had been able to practice the necessary grown-up skills called for in the moment. Consider Anna, for example, who got so frustrated by her class. Let's imagine that Anna had been able to not take the situation personally. Think how much better she would have felt about herself in this scenario, not to mention how much better she would have felt about her students.

Or let's imagine, because nobody's perfect, that Anna didn't realize what was happening to her until after the fact, but that she realized it eventually. Think of how satisfied she would feel to be able to deconstruct the scenario and recognize her role in it. Part of the reason Anna's students got so out of control is that they sensed Anna's frustration with them. Understanding this could help Anna manage and possibly prevent future class meltdowns. This realization would be a tremendous boon to any teacher, and for Anna it might have allowed her to forgive herself, forgive her students (but not necessarily let them off the hook), and maybe even take herself less seriously in the future. Doesn't such an outcome make the investment in our own growth worth it?

Or consider Joanne, who's trouble with conflict caused her more conflict in the long run. If Joanne learned to tolerate conflict and recognized that mature disagreement is healthy and not harmful, she would be able to drop her cloak of fear and stop her self-defeating behaviors. Imagine how empowered she would feel if she believed her opinions were important, and that agreement for agreement's sake kept her stunted. The only person holding Joanne back was Joanne, but with a little understanding and a little more practice, Joanne could participate more fully and positively in the life of her community. Wouldn't that be worth it?

Finally, consider Heather, who had trouble looking at herself, especially following awkward comments to her students. Had Heather been able to examine herself and take in feedback, she would have not only kept her job, she also would have gained real satisfaction at being able to do her job in increasingly more effective ways. Think of how wonderful she would have felt knowing she could adapt to her environment, incorporate constructive criticism into her work, and have a positive impact on the lives of her students.

We should commit ourselves to our own growth in the same way we encourage our students to grow. When we do so we develop self-assurance, self-confidence, competence, and resilience. If these rewards aren't enough to make growing up worth it, I don't know what is.

EXERCISES AND REFLECTIONS

1. Which of the seven grown-up skills comes easily to you? Why? Which of the skills is more challenging? Why?
2. In what aspects of your work are you most grown-up? In what aspects are you more grown-older?
3. When you were a child, what did the term *grown-up* mean to you? What constituted maturity? Who were your adult role models and why did you admire them?
4. Consider a time when you behaved with students in a less than grown-up manner. What were the circumstances? Why would you consider your behavior to be grown-older?
5. When was the last time you dealt with conflict at work? What were the circumstances, and how was the conflict resolved? How comfortable are you with conflict, and how is conflict dealt with in your school community?

6. Think about a colleague whose behavior you consider to be more grown-older than grown-up. In your estimation, what makes his or her behavior grown-older? How is his or her behavior problematic for students?

7. How would you rate your school culture in terms of grown-up behavior? Who sets the tone for behavior? How are expectations for adult behavior communicated?

8. Who do you admire at your school, and why? If you had to model your behavior on anyone at work, who would it be and what behaviors would you emulate?

9. What advice would you give to a new colleague about your school culture in terms of adult behavior? What should they know to be successful? What are some of the unwritten rules in your community about adult behavior?

10. Select one or more of the case studies from this chapter and respond to the following questions:

    a. Can you imagine being in their shoes, and if not, why not?
    b. If this were your colleague, what advice would you give them about how to deal with the situation?
    c. How should the school deal with the case in question?
    d. Which transgressions seem most serious? Which seem not as serious? Why?

CHAPTER SUMMARY

There are seven grown-up skills we should practice in order to be effective in our work with teenagers. These skills can be learned and mastered by all adults, and it is incumbent upon those of us who work in the teenage world to understand why these skills matter. The seven grown-up skills encompass the practices, attitudes, and behaviors that we should employ to maintain boundaries in our relationships with teenagers and to deal with the feverish and infectious aspects of adolescence.

NOTES

1. My understanding of being grown-up has been shaped by my work in schools and my observations of adults and their interactions with students in the teenage world.

This discussion of grown-up skills derives from this experience, and it is an important qualifier. My list of what constitutes psychological maturity may differ from another's precisely because I'm interested primarily in the dynamic between adults and teens, not just in adults themselves. The criteria for being grown-up should be understood in this context, and with the understanding that when it comes to being a grown-up in a teenage world, context is everything.

2. As I wrote this, a story about a large riot in an L.A. high school came over the wires. What started as a conflict between rival cliques turned into a school-wide brawl involving as many as 600 students. This is a prime example of how quickly the fever of adolescence can spiral out of control, in this case primarily due to lack of impulse control.

3. The law prohibiting sex between adults and minors varies from region to region. Teachers should acquaint themselves with the laws of their state and understand their responsibilities as mandated reporters of such behavior. But knowing the law isn't enough. As educators we must hold ourselves to a standard of behavior that surpasses the law. For instance, let's say Laura had been eighteen and Bill twenty-three when they got involved, not an inconceivable scenario. What then? Although the law may not prohibit such a relationship, our ethical standard does, given the power differential between teacher and student.

4

THE FIVE THINGS TEENAGERS
NEED FROM GROWN-UPS

Teenagers need five basic things from us and each of these things derives from an application of one or more of the seven grown-up skills. Teenagers need us to differentiate between their needs and their wants; to respond but not to react to them; to relate but not to identify with them; to be friendly with them but not be their friends; and to work in service of them, not of ourselves.

THE BOTTOM LINE: TEENAGERS NEED ADULTS
TO BE GROWN-UPS

I have worked with teenagers who face the most extraordinary challenges in life: Kids who live in extreme poverty or in drive-by shooting zones, or whose families are refugees. I've worked with teens whose parents are illiterate or don't speak the dominant language. I've worked with teens whose families were obliterated in the Holocaust and the Killing Fields of Cambodia.

On the flip side, I've worked with teens who come from extreme wealth and privilege, who want for literally nothing, whose parents own their own planes, footballs teams, and islands in the Caribbean. I've worked with kids who go to Bali just to learn to surf, have swimming pools on their roof decks, and own private art collections that are of museum quality.

After spending my career working with adolescents on either end of the privilege spectrum (and everywhere in between), I can say without reservation that neither severe deprivation nor the buffering effects of material privilege has a greater impact on whether they will succeed in school or in life than does the presence of at least one consistent and loving grown-up in their lives.[1]

Okay, so grown-ups are important. You get the point. But how are they important specifically? And how are they important in the teenage world? In the previous chapter, I outlined the *seven grown-up skills* we should practice to be effective with students in schools. In this chapter, I address the fundamental things teenagers need in their relationships with us, each of which requires us to practice one or more of the seven skills.

FIVE THINGS TEENAGERS NEED FROM GROWN-UPS

Teenagers need five basic things from adults who work in the teenage world. They need us to:

1. Distinguish between their needs and wants. This is Needs vs. Wants.
2. Respond to them but not react with them. This is Responding vs. Reacting.
3. Relate to them but not identify with them. This is Relating vs. Identifying.
4. Be friendly with them but not be their friends. This is Friendly vs. Friends.
5. Focus on their needs and not on our own. This is Other vs. Self.

The *five things teenagers need from grown-ups* constitute what is most essential in our relationship with teens and exist independently of the skills we must have in order to be good instructors, like knowledge of subject matter and an understanding of pedagogy. Content knowledge and pedagogy are critical components of good teaching, of course, but they do not necessarily bear upon our dynamic with teens. Thus the five things can be understood as a recipe for healthy interactions between us and our students, with each need comprising an essential ingredient of the relationship.

Need 1: Needs vs. Wants

The first thing teenagers need from adults is for us to understand the difference between their needs and their wants, and for us to satisfy their needs as opposed to their wants. This doesn't mean we should never satisfy their desires, of course, just that their needs come first and it is our job to understand what these needs are. In order to identify and prioritize teenage needs, we must practice the grown-up skills of good judgment, maintaining boundaries, and dealing with conflict.

Teenagers *want* lots of things, from iPhones to staying up all night to not doing their homework, but that doesn't mean they *need* lots of things. The teenage brain, with its developing capacity for impulse control and judgment, requires guidance. It requires help to satisfy its basic needs on the one hand, and to not be held hostage to its desires on the other. As we saw in the case of the shark girls from chapter 1, if teenagers got everything they wanted, they might get eaten alive. To avoid this fate, teens need us to protect them from shark-infested waters, or from their unbridled and potentially harmful desires.

Striking a balance between giving teens what they need and what they want is an art of sorts, one that we must practice every day in our work with teenagers. As the saying goes, when you don't get what you want, you get character. I like to add, when you don't get what you need, you get into trouble. We are responsible for keeping adolescents out of trouble in the teenage world, and for getting them back on track when they falter, and to do this we must meet their basic needs. What's the difference between a teenage need and want?

Need

A *need* is something essential, something teenagers can't live without, and it has a direct bearing on student success in the teenage world. A need is a *sine qua non* of the teenage experience at school. Most teenagers have the same basic needs.

Want

A *want* or a *desire* is something nonessential, something teenagers can live without. A want does not have bearing on teenage success in school, although it might feel like it does to the teenager in question. Teenagers have myriad desires.

Distinguishing Teenage Needs from Wants: Three Essential Questions

We must use good judgment based on the above criteria to distinguish between teenage needs and wants. In some instances, this will be an easy and straightforward process, and the distinction between the two will be clear. In others, it won't be clear at all, and it may take time to determine what's what. There are three questions we can ask ourselves that will help us clarify the issue when we're confused about teenage needs and wants. They are:

1. Does the issue at hand support learning?
2. Is it safe?
3. Is it developmentally appropriate?

If the answer to all three questions is yes, then we're probably dealing with a teenage need, and if not a need then with a desire that doesn't conflict with a need (and which can be satisfied at our discretion). If the answer to any of the above questions is no, then we're probably dealing with a teenage desire, one that we should meet only when our good judgment allows.

The Three Requirements

The three essential questions point to three basic requirements teenagers have from their experience in school. These requirements are:

1. To learn
2. To be safe and to be dealt with fairly, and to be in an environment where sound and well-reasoned discipline is practiced
3. To be understood in a developmentally appropriate manner

When these three basic requirements are met—when we can answer yes to the three essential questions—then we're meeting teenage needs and doing our jobs in schools.

A Class on the Lawn

Imagine, for a moment, that twenty students ask if they can have class outside on the lawn. It is a beautiful fall day, the school day is winding down, and there's half an hour left before dismissal. Our students start to beg us to continue the class outside. What should we do? Well, it's hard to argue that having class on the lawn is a basic need (unless the building is on fire, of course). Clearly the students *want* to go outside, they don't *need* to go outside. They are expressing a desire—that's easy to see—and maybe it's a desire we can accommodate.

Let's ask the three essential questions to clarify the issue. First, would class on the lawn satisfy our students' need to learn? This depends, and it depends on the answers to the other essential questions. Would it be safe to have class on the lawn, and can we maintain limits and discipline? In other words, can we manage the situation under such circumstances? Perhaps a strong teacher with a well-behaved class of seniors can pull it off, but what about the same teacher with rambunctious 7th graders? That's another story.[2]

Second, would class on the lawn be developmentally appropriate, and is this a reasonable desire to meet? Again, this depends on the students and the specifics of the request. Seniors and 7th graders will have very different experiences on the lawn, and their experiences will bear on their ability to learn. If we factor in these developmental issues, then we can make accommodations, like reducing the time outside for the younger kids or creating structured activities to keep them busy. As you see, it all depends on circumstances and the basic teenage requirements, which the three essential questions address.

This scenario illustrates why we must use good judgment to discern teenage needs from wants, and also how the skills of maintaining boundaries and dealing with conflict come into play. Let's say we deny our students' request to go outside, in part because we know we won't be able to maintain appropriate control of the group once we get there. Here we use good judgment to evaluate our ability to practice our other grown-up skills, namely, maintaining boundaries. But once we make this decision, we may have to deal with the conflict that arises from denying our students' request.

And so it goes. A simple student request plunges us into the complications of the teenage world, where our ability to discriminate between teenage needs and wants is essential.

Need 2: Responding vs. Reacting

The second thing teenagers need is to be surrounded by adults who can respond *to* them and not react *with* them. This need relates to the practice of a number of grown-up skills including self-awareness, the ability to tolerate conflict, and most importantly self-control and self-mastery. Teenagers need us to be able to respond differently than they do because they literally don't have the brain power to control themselves at times. Teenagers need us to be their brakes, not their accelerators, so to speak, as they career about on the teenage journey.

For our purposes, responding is our ability to approach situations in a reasoned manner, without reacting with a knee jerk. Reacting is just the opposite: It *is* a knee jerk, and it's often how the teenage brain operates. Sometimes teenagers don't respond because they simply can't—they only can react—which is why those of us who work with them must respond to them and not react with them.

The Three-Second Delay

The *three-second delay* is a term I use to describe the differences between responding and reacting, and between the teenage and adult brains. The three-second delay is the period during which we pause, step back, and consider our response to the situation. During this delay, we use our prefrontal cortex to assess the situation and to determine an appropriate course of action. In other words, we use impulse control. When we react, on the other hand, we behave without thinking, or by thinking like our students. When we react, we exercise no impulse control and our brains function like teenage brains. Should we take the three-second delay literally? No, actual response times are not important, it's what's happening in the adult brain and the intention of the response that matter.

For an example of the three-second delay, or lack thereof, let's return to the vignette from chapter 2 in which a group of teachers got caught up in the frenzy surrounding a student who claimed she was being bullied. The teachers immediately made the assumption that the student in question had characterized the situation accurately. If the student said she was being bullied, then she was being bullied, or so they reasoned. The teachers involved did not investigate further, nor did they question the other students or seek alternative explanations for the situation. They took one student's account at face value. In the end, they didn't employ the three-second delay: They reacted, they didn't respond.

Now, let me be clear. I do not believe the student in question was lying or overreacting. She believed she was being picked on and bullied, and her feelings were genuine. What I am suggesting, and what I believe to be true, is that the adults who were involved reacted immediately to allegations without ever exploring other sides of the story precisely because their student's reaction was so heartfelt. They reacted to the situation the same way she did, which was without the three-second delay. The student, of course, couldn't use this technique; she hadn't developed the brain capacity to do so. But her teachers presumably had, and yet they didn't because they got swept up in the teenage moment.

Had they employed the delay, which is what their students needed them to do, they would have discovered that the situation was not as clear-cut as they thought. While it was true that their student felt hurt, and that some other students didn't like her (and she didn't like them), there was an additional truth that got lost in the midst of the adult reaction: The upset student was having a typical teenage reaction to a typical teenage social situation. Her brain was reacting and not responding to what was going on, and she needed help from the adults around her to deal with this inner reality, not just the outer one.

Current Climate of Reactivity

In our current social climate, it can be difficult for us *not* to jump to conclusions, like these teachers did, when certain allegations are made. When terms like *harassment* or *bullying* are leveled against anyone in schools, we are quick to react, sometimes too quick. Before I continue, let me state that I do not support bullying or harassment of any kind. That said, I also don't support adults jumping on bandwagons or jumping to conclusions when it involves students.

Entire school communities and our society at large, really, are currently in the grip of this reactive stance when it comes to adolescent behavior. When allegations of bullying or harassment are made, or when students feel hurt, adults tend to react quickly and often without thinking. At times, we practice little self-control or self-awareness when we suspect someone is being bullied because we fear that any hesitation on our part will be perceived as being unsupportive of the "victim." This is an honest mistake given the current social climate, but it's one we should recognize for what it is: a knee-jerk reaction, when a disinterested response is what we need in order to understand and resolve the situation effectively.

We should resist our desire to react when it comes to disputes between our students, and instead we should respond with fairness, dispassion, and even-mindedness. When we don't, we risk confusing our own emotional reactions with our students', and then we end up responding in kind. Of course, when bullying or harassment is occurring we must intervene accordingly, but an appropriate response is never a reactive one. The truth is, in situations where true bullying or harassment occur, teenagers need our capacity to respond more than ever.

The Case of Lizzie

Lizzie's case offers another example of reaction versus response, albeit a less dramatic one. Lizzie was a popular teacher noted for her empathy for students. One day Lizzie was approached by Angelica, a student in her algebra class. Angelica was upset about a grade she received on her mid-term exam, and as she spoke with Lizzie, she started to cry. Angelica told Lizzie she feared telling her parents about her grade because they had very high expectations for her (both of her parents had done well in algebra, something they reminded her of at every turn, or so it seemed to Angelica).

Despite her experience, Lizzie felt increasingly overwhelmed during her conversation with Angelica. She started to see the world through Angelica's eyes: disapproving parents, grim future, homelessness as a direct result of a poor algebra grade (I'm only half-joking). Lizzie tried every trick in the book to console Angelica, but when nothing seemed to work she did the only thing she could think of: She raised Angelica's grade.

This is what happens when we react and fail to respond: We throw caution to the wind. Not surprisingly, when Lizzie acquiesced to Angelica's plea for mercy, Angelica felt better. But Lizzie's reaction did not solve the situation. In fact, it made it worse. When Lizzie finally came to her senses and switched on her three-second delay, she realized what she had done and had to clean up her mess.

This is what reactions are like; they're messy and it's our job to clean them up. If Lizzie hadn't cleaned up her own mess, somebody else would have had to, most probably Angelica herself. And we should all clean up our own mess. When we practice grown-up skills in the teenage world, especially the skill of self-control, we make our lives much easier for ourselves, and we have a lot less mess to clean up at the end of the day.

Every teacher I know has a tale to tell about reacting instead of responding. This may be the most common challenge we face in our work, especially for new teachers. Teenagers are highly reactive, and because we spend so much time with them it makes sense that we are reactive at times too. When we are immersed in the teenage world, reacting can start to feel natural, which is why it is so important for us to appreciate the differences between responding and reacting, and to develop good habits of response.

Need 3: Relating vs. Identifying

The third thing teenagers need is for us to relate *to* them, not to identify *with* them. Lizzie, in her moment of reactivity, identified with Angelica's plight, so much so that she couldn't see beyond Angelica's perspective to find a viable solution to the problem at hand. Because Lizzie identified with Angelica, she missed the opportunity to relate to her and help her solve her problem in an appropriate way. For example, rather than getting caught up in Angelica's emotion, Lizzie might have engaged her in a conversation about her relationship with her parents and their expectations, and even offered to help Angelica talk to her parents about how she was doing in school.

The distinction between relating to and identifying with teenagers is a critical aspect of the adult-teenager relationship. When we relate to teenagers, we connect to them but continue to see them as separate from us; we don't project our issues onto them. When we identify with teenagers, on the other hand, we confuse their experiences with our own, and as a result we see our ourselves in them, and vice versa.

When we relate to teenagers, we practice the grown-up skills of self-awareness, self-control, good judgment, and good boundaries. When we identify with teenagers, we blur the boundaries between our own experience and theirs, and our grown-up skills get left by the wayside.

Empathy vs. Sympathy

One way to understand how relating to students differs from identifying with them is to consider the distinction between empathy and sympathy. Although these terms don't offer a perfect parallel, they come close, and I find them useful when it comes to understanding what teenagers need from adults.

Sympathy is the "inclination to think or feel alike . . . [and] a mutual or parallel susceptibility,"[3] which is what occurred for Lizzie as she dealt with Angelica. Lizzie started to feel the same way Angelica did, and she reacted to the situation based on these sympathetic feelings. This idea of a mutual or parallel susceptibility captures our vulnerability in the face of teenage drama, as Lizzie's reaction to Angelica demonstrates. All of us are susceptible to teenagers in this way, and thus to getting swept up in their world; and we know we are identifying *with* teenagers and not relating *to* them when we start to think or feel the same way they do.

Empathy, in contrast, is the "action of understanding, being aware of, being sensitive to, and vicariously experiencing the feelings, thoughts, and experience of another." Sounds similar, doesn't it? Here's the major difference, though, and it's subtle. Empathy suggests a response that allows for the discrimination between self and other in the moment. An empathic response remains at a remove. A sympathetic response doesn't, and during a sympathetic response we focus as much attention on ourselves as on the other person, if not more.

When we relate to teenagers, we have empathy for them. When we identify with teenagers, we have sympathy for them, if that. With empathy, we keep our own perspective and vantage point; with sympathy we don't—we get a little too close for comfort and, when this happens, we risk confusing our students' problems with our own.

It's Not About Age

You might think younger adults would be more susceptible than older ones to identifying with teenagers, but this is not necessarily the case. While there is a period during which young adults must develop grown-up skills, age doesn't make a difference after this initial adjustment period is over. This is an important point to remember when we consider the differences between relating to and identifying with teens. It's not about age.

The Case of Pam

Pam's story illustrates this point. Pam was only a few years out of nursing school when she got a position as the school nurse at a large urban high school. Part of her job was to work closely with the school's peer leaders and direct them in their work with younger students. Pam inherited a program that students perceived as accessible and casual; her predecessor had deemphasized the boundary between herself and her students. For someone without Pam's grown-up skills and good boundaries, an office complete with couches, cushions, and condoms could have been a recipe for disaster. But Pam had no trouble with it. She was professional, approachable, and her students loved her because she related to them so well.

Some of Pam's colleagues believed Pam's skill at relating to her students was a function of her age, but they were mistaken. Pam was effective in her work with teenagers precisely because she didn't identify with them, she related to them, a skill that had nothing to do with how old she was. Pam could effectively separate her own experiences from those of her students; she empathized with her students, which allowed her to relate to their experiences and connect to them in a grown-up way.

The Case of Gianna Redux

Gianna's story, from chapter 3, provides another example of the relative unimportance of age as it pertains to relating to versus identifying with students. Gianna, an experienced teacher in her late thirties, was unable to relate to the students in her sexuality class. Instead, she identified with them and as a result she didn't maintain the boundaries that should have existed between them.

Because she identified with her students, and because they urged her to self-disclose, Gianna assumed her students would benefit from hearing about her own life story and sexual history, and that this would make them feel comfortable and encourage discussion. This might have been true had Gianna's relationship with her audience been reciprocal, but it wasn't. Despite the encouragement she got from her students, many of them felt uncomfortable when Gianna shared her story. They were unable to relate to Gianna because she didn't relate to them, at least not until she got some assistance.

Gianna's case underscores the need for adults to practice self-awareness, good judgment, and maintain good boundaries in order to relate to students and not to identify with them. Gianna's situation also underscores the need for administrators to be clear with teachers about what they expect in terms of behavior. Gianna's department chair eventually made it clear to Gianna, but this conversation came after the fact. We, along with Gianna, need guidance and direction *before* we enter the classroom, and possibly throughout the process. Especially when we teach controversial or value-laden subjects, like sexuality, it's helpful for administrators to actively mentor teachers and for teachers to support each other as challenges with boundaries arise in the classroom.

Need 4: Being Friendly vs. Being Friends

The fourth thing teenagers need from us is our ability to understand the difference between being friendly with them and being their friend. Gianna saw her students as peers, and she wanted to treat them as equals. The relationship between us and teenagers can never be equal, though, and *being friendly vs. being friends* addresses this reality.

A critical difference between being friendly and being friends is that friendly is an attitude, it's a stance. We can be friendly with anyone. Friendship, on the other hand, is a relationship with implied expectations and presumed mutuality. We can't be friends with everyone. More importantly, friendship implies a degree of give-and-take that can't exist in a relationship in which there is a power differential, like there is in the student-teacher relationship. Friendship between adults and teenagers in schools, therefore, is categorically out of the question.

When we practice the grown-up skills of self-awareness, good judgment, and an ability to maintain boundaries we ensure that our relationships with teenagers remain friendly in the teenage world, and don't cross the line into friendship.

One Person's Friendly Is Another Person's Friend

A student once described to me his relationship with his favorite teacher. He listed all the things he liked about his teacher and described how much he enjoyed his class. He said he admired his teacher for all kinds of reasons, and added that he wanted to become a teacher himself because of the fine example his own teacher had set. Then he said his teacher was one of his best friends.

Not a problem, as long as the teacher didn't say the same thing. Students have all kinds of reactions to their teachers, and one of them may be a desire for their friendship. No harm was done when this student described his teacher as a friend, but harm could have been done if the teacher had responded in the same way. Luckily, the teacher in question understood what was going on. He accepted his student's feelings for him and made certain to maintain the boundary between them. He was friendly with his student and didn't confuse being friendly with being a friend.

But let's say he had. Let's say this teacher *had* confused being friendly with being friends and had treated his student accordingly. What could happen then, and why would it be so bad?

To review, friendship implies reciprocity, something that does not and cannot exist between teenagers and adults in the teenage world. As adults, we have ultimate authority over teens at school, and this power is a barrier to friendship. If we considered teenagers our friends, we would never be able to exert our authority over them when we need to, which is pretty much all day, every day. Imagine trying to exert authority over your adult friends. It wouldn't work, and if it did it would imply either that the relationship wasn't really a friendship, or that authority between friends was shared depending on the circumstance. This is another reason why friendship between adults and teenagers in schools can't work: There is never a circumstance during which teenagers have ultimate authority over adults in schools, and if they do, something is wrong.

The Case of Tony

Tony was a young, inexperienced humanities teacher who supervised the yearbook. Tony was lonely much of the time, so he looked forward

to hanging out with students after school as they worked on the yearbook. Tony didn't mind if deadlines caused the staff to stay late or work
on weekends; hanging out with his students was the extent of his social
life. In an effort to keep his students happy, Tony always bought food
and other incentives to keep them working, and to make them like him.
Tony didn't see his behavior or feelings as problematic; he even bragged
to his colleagues about how close he was to his yearbook staff and that
they were his friends.

Okay, so what's wrong with a lonely guy thinking his students are his
friends? Well, for starters, it was a complete misread of the situation.
None of Tony's students saw him as a friend, they saw him for what he
was: a guy who tried to curry favor with them. Second, as a result, Tony
was quite ineffectual at his job, which was to guide and supervise his
students. The teenagers ran the show, and Tony could no more rein
them in than he could understand his own behavior. When things inevitably got out of control, Tony was at a loss—he didn't want to alienate
or anger his "friends" by setting limits.

In addition to his inability to do his job effectively, Tony made his
students feel uncomfortable. His need for their approval and attention
was palpable, and his students found it off-putting. Tony's students accepted his food but rejected everything else he offered them because
they understood on some level how inappropriate his desire for their
friendship was. But let's say one of them had accepted Tony's offer of
friendship. What then?

When we cross the line and view teenagers as friends, the burden
on the teenager is huge. Teenagers are not capable of dealing with our
problems, and when we consider teenagers to be our friends we have a
problem. Teenagers have enough problems of their own, so they can't
reasonably deal with our life circumstances. Teenagers aren't developmentally ready to take on our burdens and one of the things friends do
is share their burdens.

Tony shared his burden of loneliness with his students and, understandably, they couldn't do anything about it: It wasn't their responsibility. If a student had accepted Tony's offer of friendship, he or she would
have been sucked into a chasm of unmet adult needs that would engulf
them both, and this could seriously compromise the teenager's ability to
get his or her own needs met.

Chances are also good that such a student would suffer consequences from his or her peers, most probably in the form of derision or exclusion. Nobody likes a teacher's pet, and when adults act like their students' friends, we set students up and do them a serious disservice when it comes to the student's peer relationships. When we think students are our friends, we play favorites, another challenge in the teenage world.

Tony was not alone in feeling isolated in his work. Working with teenagers all day can be a very lonely enterprise. We can't share ourselves with teenagers the way they share themselves with us, and this can leave us at a loss. But this is the reality of our work, and it can be very challenging at times. Most adults seek companionship at work, it's natural. But those of us who work in the teenage world can't, at least not from our students.

When we start to feel lonely, we should reach out to other adults and talk about our experience. Chances are good they will have similar stories to share. Administrators should be on the lookout for teachers who seem isolated or not integrated with their colleagues, and they should pay close attention to new or young teachers who may not feel comfortable reaching out for help. There are many of us who share Tony's struggles with loneliness and lack of connection, and if our communities are receptive to our plight, this will go a long way to solving the problem. We need to make our communities sympathetic to hazards such as loneliness, otherwise we may look to students for companionship and start playing favorites, which puts us, and them, in an untenable position.

Having Favorites vs. Playing Favorites

All adults who work with teenagers have favorites; it's not just the Tonys of the world. I repeat, *all* adults who work in the teenage world have favorites, and this is important for us to admit (not to our students, of course). Students are different and therefore we react to them differently. This is normal. But having favorites and playing favorites are also different, and playing favorites can lead to trouble.

The slippery slope that runs from being friendly with students to being their friends (or to acting like their friends, shall we say) begins with the fact that adults have favorites. Adults who practice grown-up skills can live with the reality that we have favorites, whereas grown-older adults give into the temptation to play favorites. Playing favorites is a temptation because when we play favorites we are less interested in expressing favoritism than we are in being favored ourselves. Playing favorites, therefore, is about *being* a favorite, not just about having one, and this is tempting for all of us.

The Case of Doug

Playing favorites can take many forms. For Doug, it meant having a particularly close relationship with the star players on his baseball team. The year Doug's team did well in their league, Doug became attached to three of his best players, and they to him. Doug was rightfully proud of their accomplishments, and he often singled his players out for attention and special treatment. He made sure he highlighted their achievements in public whenever he got the chance. Doug was determined that the whole school would see just how great his players were.

Most of us are proud of our students' accomplishments, and this is how it started out for Doug. But things changed, and gradually Doug's interest in his players had more to do with meeting his own needs for attention than it did with his pride as a coach. The more attention he gave, the more attention he got, and this made the cycle hard to recognize and break. Doug continued to publicly fete his players well beyond what they deserved, and well beyond what his other players could tolerate.

Another danger of playing favorites is the inevitable effect it has on the not favored student. Most teenagers are generous enough to accept when their peers get recognition that is deserved. Most teenagers are also smart enough to recognize when attention goes beyond what is merited. This is what happened with Doug's players, the unsung ones, who came to realize that Doug wasn't playing fair. They knew their teammates were great, but also they knew they weren't *that* great, and this changed their opinion of Doug.

The Seduction of Being Favored

Being favored by teenagers is seductive. I'm not suggesting teenagers themselves are seductive but the attention they give can be. Such attention can tempt almost any adult into cultivating relationships that extend beyond the bounds of friendliness. Teenagers, in their desire to get close to their favorite adults, may unwittingly encourage adults to treat them differently, as Doug's players did. Doug's players fawned over him in the same way he fawned over them, and while the relationship they formed wasn't one of equals, it was one of equal attention and intensity. This kind of mutual admiration is hard to resist unless it is seen for what it is, and resist it we must.

Doug could have untangled himself from his predicament by evaluating how much energy he was expending on each of his players' behalf. When we determine that some students are getting more from us than others, we need to evaluate the situation.[4] Doug didn't need to back off from his favored students as much as he needed to include other students into his sphere of attention. Such a shift in emphasis would have reduced the intensity of some of his attachments and increased the intensity of others, thus balancing out his attention expenditure. As all teachers know, we have only so much attention to give, and it's our duty to spread this attention among our students as evenly as possible. When we focus on spending our attention evenly, this helps us avoid the pitfalls of playing favorites and of joining in the teenage world.

Joining vs. Joining In

A wise teacher pointed out to me the distinction between joining teenagers and joining *in* with teenagers.[5] *Joining* implies behaving with teenagers in a friendly, grown-up manner. *Joining in* implies behaving with teens in an identified, friend-like, grown-older way. Doug joined in and when he did, he shifted the focus from his players to himself, and from their needs to his own.

When we understand the difference between joining and joining in with teenagers, and when we resist the temptation to play favorites and to be favored by teenagers, we can maintain the boundary between being friendly with students and being their friends. In the process, we'll be more effective educators and happier adults.

Need 5: Serving the Other vs. Serving the Self

All of the above teenage needs are connected to this final one, the need for adults in the teenage world to work primarily in the service of others and not of ourselves. This means teens need us to prioritize their needs over our own, at least when it comes to our work with them. The grown-up skill of self-transcendence is of paramount importance here, but the skills of good judgment, self-awareness, and self-control are also important.

The Grown-Up Paradox

In order to put others first we must take care of ourselves, and this is what I call the *grown-up paradox*. I use the term *paradox* because taking care of ourselves and teenagers at the same time is hard to do, especially for adults new to the teenage world. Teenage needs often seem endless, and meeting them can be exhausting, and adult self-care may go by the wayside in the face of teenage demands.

But we all must rise to the challenge of the grown-up paradox. If we don't, we risk one of two outcomes: Either we lose ourselves in the needs of our students and become martyrs, or we focus too much on ourselves and become narcissistic. Most adults in the teenage world don't get this out of balance, but it can happen if we're not careful. I will return to the issue of adult self-care in detail in chapter 7; for now, it's important that we understand our mandate to put others first while maintaining a basic level of self-care in the process.

The Case of Sandy

Sandy had trouble with the grown-up paradox. Sandy was a language arts teacher who always put her students first. She was professional and kind, and devoted to her job to the exclusion of everything else, including her health. During one long and snowy winter, Sandy contracted a nasty infection that wouldn't go away. Despite her illness, Sandy thought it was her duty to continue to work even when she felt terrible and, unfortunately for her, many of her colleagues didn't understand the severity of her situation.

Sandy never considered taking time off to heal. She didn't value her own health enough to understand that this would benefit her students in the long run. Instead, she kept teaching until she could no longer function, at which point she was forced to take several weeks off of work to recover.

Teenagers need adults to model self-care. They learned the opposite from Sandy, who instead modeled self-abnegation. Sandy's behavior was problematic because she didn't understand that she was responsible for attending to her own legitimate needs in addition to those of her students—she thought her students were all that mattered, and paradoxically she didn't understand that her behavior was in fact discounting their need (to have a healthy teacher). She also made the mistake of thinking she was irreplaceable, a mistake many of us make in our work. She believed that if she didn't come to work, regardless of how sick she was, her students would be left hanging. No doubt her absence would have had an effect on them, but it wouldn't have been detrimental if it had been in the service of legitimate self-care.

Sandy had a hard time practicing the skill of self-transcendence. Despite her dedication to her students, at heart she couldn't transcend her own need to feel irreplaceable. But beneath this sentiment, Sandy really feared she *was* replaceable, and that if she took care of her own needs she wouldn't be needed in return. Sandy could have used the support of an astute supervisor to let her know that she was both replaceable, in that her students would survive a few days without her, and irreplaceable, in that she was an important member of the community. In making her daily work solely about her students, Sandy lost sight of her own importance and her unique contributions to her community.

The Critical Question: Who Does This Serve?

Sandy's situation illustrates the delicate balance we must strike between taking care of ourselves and taking care of others. This is an endless challenge, so we must regularly examine our behavior and motives to ensure we are acting in service of our students. One way to do this is to ask ourselves the question, Who does this serve? when we consider our actions. The answer should be: our students. If it isn't, then we must reexamine our behavior and intentions and determine how to get ourselves back on track. When we take care of students in this way we ultimately take care of ourselves, because what's in our students' best interests is almost always in our own best interests too, and this is what Sandy needed help to understand.

The Case of LeAnn

LeAnn needed to ask herself this critical question, and she needed to pay attention to the answer because her actions did not ultimately serve her students. LeAnn was a veteran teacher with over thirty years of experience, and she was tired, perhaps even burned out. But LeAnn liked teaching for lots of reasons (can you say summer?), and so she stayed in the profession. But her heart wasn't in it anymore and it showed.

Because she didn't feel invested anymore, LeAnn didn't do her best. She didn't revise her lesson plans regularly or think much about what she was going to teach; she had the expertise and experience to just show up and go through the motions. She also didn't have the energy to involve herself with her students outside the classroom. As a result, she didn't stay on campus after school despite the fact that she was contractually required to do so. LeAnn left school when her last class was finished, and departed by a back entrance in the hope that no one would notice her departure. But people did notice—especially her students, who couldn't find her when they had questions or needed help.

LeAnn was so exhausted she could think only of herself. Tired as we might get in the teenage world, none of us who works with adolescents has this luxury. LeAnn's idea of self-care, like leaving school early, made sense on the surface, but ultimately her coping strategies didn't serve her or her students. LeAnn's efforts never brought back her energy or enthusiasm for work, and so everyone was left wanting. LeAnn needed more than an early departure from work to solve her problems; she needed to examine whether she wanted to do the hard work of teaching anymore. If she did, then she needed to determine how she could prioritize her students' needs and serve them effectively without feeling so depleted.

All of us have days when we prioritize our own needs but LeAnn did this most days and, when this happens, it's a sign we should rethink what we're doing. Perhaps LeAnn needed a sabbatical, or maybe she needed to leave the profession altogether. It is not heretical for a teacher to consider a career change, and it's something administrators should talk about as an option when they deal with someone like LeAnn, who just didn't have it in her anymore. Acknowledging our own burnout can be one of the best ways we serve our students, who otherwise get the brunt of our tired and depleted selves.

The Case of Grant

Unlike LeAnn, Grant was very invested in the welfare of his students. He regularly met with every student outside of class as an expression of this commitment, but he often engaged in conversations that went beyond the bounds of the teacher-student relationship. Admittedly, Grant was a good listener, so students were quick to reveal themselves to him, but he also was quick to disclose personal information back.

Grant openly shared details of his own struggles during high school, which included dealing with undiagnosed attention deficit disorder (ADD), and he developed a following of kids who faced similar challenges. Grant became the self-proclaimed campus expert on helping kids with attention difficulties, and he considered his personal experience to be sufficient qualification for this role. This brought him into conflict with the school's learning specialist, among others, who was troubled by Grant's investment in labeling and helping students with problems beyond his area of expertise, and by doing so without collaborating with his colleagues.

Grant's concerns for his students were legitimate, but had he asked himself the question, Who does this serve?, his answer might have surprised him. In the guise of serving others, and certainly with the intention of doing so, Grant was dealing with his own issues as much as anyone's. Grant felt special in his self-designated role of expert, something he'd never felt in high school. He identified a lot with his struggling students, but this identification often overrode his ability to help them. What they needed from Grant was his help as a teacher, not as an ADD expert, but this was hard for Grant to understand. His desire to help was so strong that sometimes it clouded his judgment.

Beware Territoriality

How can we presume to understand Grant's motives, and by extension to determine if they were in the service of his needs or those of his students? The most important clue lies in his relationship with other adults within the community. Grant didn't work with his colleagues to support his students. Grant established his territory with students and became upset when others "trespassed." For instance, this happened once when a student talked with him about the work she was doing with the school's learning specialist. Grant questioned the methods of his colleague, leaving his student feeling confused about who she should listen to. In his effort to support his student, he unintentionally undermined her ability to trust her caregivers.

Grant needed to work with his colleagues, not against them; helping students is a collaborative effort in schools, and when we get territorial it's a sign that we're putting our own needs first, and not our students'. When we treat students or their problems as private property, this is a sign that students' needs are getting trumped. Grant was fortunate to have an assistant principal who helped him recognize that his method of helping his students needed to be revised. Eventually Grant was able to see that he needed to play a different role with students when it came to their learning challenges, and that once his students got the help they needed from the appropriate sources, he could still be a valuable support to them as an understanding teacher.

BACK TO THE BOTTOM LINE

Our job in the teenage world is to meet the needs of our students. This is the bottom line. While our own situations will always inform how we approach our students' needs, as we saw in Grant's case, the fact is we must put our students first and figure out how to take care of ourselves in the process. Teenagers need us to understand their needs, to respond to their needs dispassionately, and to separate our own experiences from theirs. This is perhaps the most important work we do in schools, and without it teenagers are left alone and helpless. When we practice grown-up skills, we guide teenagers and help them deal with the phenomenon of adolescence and their developing teenage brains.

EXERCISES AND REFLECTIONS

1. Consider a situation with students in which you were torn between meeting a need and a want. What was the need? What was the want? How did you resolve the situation?
2. Consider a time when you reacted to a situation with students. What happened? What aspects of the situation caused you to react and not to respond? What could you have done differently?

3. Consider a time when a colleague reacted instead of responded to a situation involving a student. What happened? How did the situation get resolved? How would the outcome of the situation have differed if your colleague had responded instead of reacted?

4. What aspects of the teenage experience do you identify with? How does this identification with your students affect your ability to relate to them as a grown-up? (You may want to consider your own adolescent experience as you think about this question, and what aspects of your experience remind you of your current work with teenagers.)

5. Who are your favorite students and why? How do you express your favoritism? Which students do you dislike and why? (If you're doing this exercise with colleagues, I suggest you refrain from sharing names of specific students. You can instead discuss the qualities you like or dislike about the students in question.)

6. Consider a situation in which you played favorites with a student. What happened? How did your behavior change with your favored student? Consider a situation in which your behavior changed because of your dislike for a student. What happened?

7. When have you been singled out as a favorite by a student? How did this feel? If you don't think you've ever been favored, consider a situation in which a colleague has been obviously favored. How did you know your colleague was being favored and how did your colleague respond?

8. What are your motives for teaching? What rewards or incentives do you get from teaching? How might your motives interfere with your ability to put the needs of your students ahead of your own?

9. When have you felt tired or disengaged from your work? What did this look like? How did you deal with it? To whom did you turn for support or guidance?

CHAPTER SUMMARY

It is the job of adults who work in the teenage world to attend to the basic needs of students, and to do this we must practice grown-up skills. Teenagers need adults to practice grown-up skills above all else, and when we do this we rise to the challenge of putting our students' needs before our own. Teenagers need us to respond to them with dispassion; to separate our own experiences from theirs; to relate to them in a friendly way without confusing this with being their friend; and to take care of ourselves so that our work can ultimately be in the service of others.

NOTES

1. I don't mean to suggest that issues such as poverty, abuse, or racism have no effect on a child's development; they do. My point is that the absence of a loving grown-up is generally more detrimental to a child's development than these other, clearly significant variables.

2. I wouldn't take my 7th graders outside during class to save my life, but that may say more about my classroom management skills (or lawn management skills, as it were) than anything else.

3. Merriam-Webster Online Dictionary, 2008.

4. There are always circumstances in which some students need more from us than others. I'm not referring here to the situations that occur routinely in the course of our teaching. I'm referring instead to those instances when our need for treating students specially overrides the demands of the situation.

5. Thanks to E. J. Katz, who got this nugget in 2007 from the Stanley H. King Counseling Institute for Independent Secondary Schools and passed it on to me.

5

DO'S AND DON'TS FOR ADULTS IN THE TEENAGE WORLD

Adults in the teenage world are responsible for maintaining boundaries in our relationships with students. The do's and don'ts in this chapter cover behavior that we should either practice or avoid to keep these boundaries in place. We are also responsible for establishing a healthy school community, and as such we must be mindful not only of our own behavior but also of how we support our colleagues and institutions as a whole.

THE DO'S AND DON'TS

Throughout this chapter, I propose fifteen guidelines for behavior that we should either avoid (don'ts) or practice (do's) in an effort to maintain healthy relationships with teenagers. Some of these behaviors are very specific and not open to interpretation (for instance, don't have sex with students), while others are more general and contextual (for example, don't lend personal things to students). Each behavior speaks to some aspect of our relationships with our students, and all of them, when practiced in combination, keep us firmly in the grown-up camp in the teenage world. The fifteen guidelines are:

Don'ts

1. Don't do anything you wouldn't want your principal to know about
2. Don't touch or have sex with students, and don't talk with students about sex
3. Don't talk about personal business with students
4. Don't communicate with students via personal email or phone, text or instant message, Facebook, or at your home
5. Don't lend or borrow personal things from students
6. Don't spend time with students after hours
7. Don't consume or discuss alcohol or drugs in the proximity of students
8. Don't talk with students about colleagues
9. Don't keep student secrets
10. Don't go beyond the scope of your role

Do's

1. Do understand and follow school policies, procedures, and best practices
2. Do seek assistance when you get overwhelmed in your relationships with teenagers
3. Do establish strong ties with colleagues
4. Do support the grown-up team within the school community
5. Do get a life

IMAGINE YOURSELF ON THE WITNESS STAND

When I work with new teachers, I advise them to imagine themselves on the witness stand, being cross-examined about their behavior involving students. I know it's dramatic but all drama aside it's a good way to instill a sense of caution in those starting out in the profession. When we work in the teenage world we must understand not only what we do with students but also why we do it, and we should be able to provide a rationale for all of our decisions. In other words, we should be able to imagine ourselves on the witness stand, defending our actions and ourselves in a reasonable manner.

The fact is the students we work with in middle and high school are children—*children*—and therefore our behavior with them must be beyond reproach, or pretty close to it most of the time. New teachers need to know this and veteran teachers need to be reminded of it in order to protect students and us. The reality is that regardless of our good intentions, all of us make mistakes with students because at some point all of us get knocked off balance by the phenomenon of adolescence. Given that mistakes are inevitable, it's good practice to think about our behavior and its repercussions on a regular basis, and to have some clear and specific guidelines that govern our actions.

This is what the do's and don'ts are for; they are about what we should and shouldn't do in our work with teenagers in schools. Most of the guidelines are plain common sense, although that doesn't mean they're easy to follow. But follow them we should because when we do, we increase our effectiveness in our work, maintain good boundaries between our students and us, and avoid the witness stand altogether.

IT'S ALL ABOUT BOUNDARIES

I haven't used the term *boundaries* much thus far because I think it gets overused in the conversation about adult behavior in schools, and subsequently I think it can be easily ignored, misunderstood, or dismissed. But make no mistake, this is what we're taking about here: boundaries. Boundaries are what adults need to establish and maintain in schools, and boundaries are what students need to stay within. Boundaries are what separate us from our students, and boundaries are what protect us from behaving like grown-olders. Without boundaries, no one is safe in schools.

The do's and don'ts can be understood, then, as guidelines or rules that articulate these boundaries and help us to maintain healthy relationships with our students. While there are exceptions to most rules, when we follow these guidelines we can rest assured that we are protecting our students and ourselves. Most of these rules don't appear in any faculty handbook, although they probably should because everyone pays the price when we don't adhere to them.

As you read through the do's and don'ts, I encourage you to consider these guidelines from two perspectives. First, I invite you to think about how each one pertains to you personally. You might ask yourself, How does this directive apply to me?, or, Is this something I struggle with? Second, I encourage you to consider how each guideline pertains to you as a member of the grown-up community at your school. You might ask yourself, What is my responsibility if a colleague is struggling to maintain one of these boundaries? What should I do and how can I support my students, my colleagues, and the community in the process? Our job is to foster a healthy community in the teenage world, not only to deal with our individual students, and this means we must help each other when we face challenges in our relationships with teenagers. It also implies that our colleagues' struggles are our own.

Administrators can help teachers enormously with the following do's and don'ts by being clear about what they expect from adults within their community. Administrators should not assume teachers have thought about these guidelines. Whereas it is the entire community's responsibility to consider these practices, it is the administrator's responsibility to make sure everyone understands what's expected of them. Sometimes it is as simple as reminding teachers that working with teenagers is challenging, and that nobody is perfect. When administrators create an atmosphere where adults can talk about their challenges, this goes a long way to preventing problematic situations from spiraling out of control.

DON'TS

The following don'ts are the ten things we should avoid in our relationships with teenagers. Each don't is concrete and fairly specific but at the same time points to a larger mandate about maintaining a healthy distance from our students. If you find yourself dismissing a particular guideline because it seems too specific or because you don't think it applies to you, I urge you to think about the issue in broader terms, until it has some meaning for you personally. The more we relate each don't to our own experience, whether it is from a personal perspective or from our vantage point as a member of the community, the more fruitful our examination of our behavior will be, and by extension the more we will contribute to a healthy school community.

I. Don't Do Anything You Wouldn't Want Your Principal to Know About

We shouldn't do anything we don't want our principals to know about. What goes around comes around in schools, so we should guide our behavior with the thought that everything we do can and will get back to our supervisor, or to someone else. There are no secrets in the teenage world, so we should behave accordingly. Whether it's the image of the witness stand or of our principal looming over our shoulder, it's good to have a way to remember that our behavior is transparent when we work in schools.

Another way to think about this is to remember that our work in schools is in the public domain. Unless we have the legal right to have confidential conversations with students, as do the school nurse and counselor in some jurisdictions,[1] everything we say or do is up for scrutiny (and even when we do have the legal right to maintain confidentiality, the other person in the conversation can say whatever they want about us). Just keep in mind that our work and behavior in schools is an open book, and this is how it should be. When we use this notion of transparency as our guide, we are better teachers, better colleagues, and more effective community members. Like all of the other don'ts, this one is meant to improve our experience at work, and the experience of everyone else around us.

2. Don't Touch or Have Sex with Students, and Don't Talk to Students about Sex

This one is fairly obvious, isn't it? Everyone knows about this one. There's not much more to say, is there?

When Children Are Targeted Sexually by Adults in Schools

Sadly, there is a lot to say about this guideline because apparently adults target students sexually in schools more often than we might suspect, and certainly more often than we'd like to believe or admit. In 2004, the U.S. Department of Education commissioned a study to survey and synthesize the literature on the prevalence of "educator sexual misconduct" in American schools.[2] The results are disturbing. According to the data, upwards of 10 percent of American school children have been targeted in a sexual manner by adults who work in schools. The majority of students targeted are female (56–77 percent, depending on the study) and the majority of offenders are male (57–90 percent, depending on the study). In addition, male and female adults have targeted students of the same gender at a lower but still significant rate (15 percent male to male, 13 percent female to female). And of course, adult women target male students, too. It's all bad.

To make matters worse, the study claims that many offenders "are those most celebrated in their profession."[3] This suggests that adults who engage in sexual misconduct in schools might not arouse the suspicions of their colleagues. They might not be creepy or recognizably disturbed, or be loners with poor social skills (although having these attributes does not mean someone is an offender, by any means). A colleague of a distinguished department chair who had a long-standing affair with one of his female students, said of him, "He's absolutely the last guy I would suspect of something like this."

So, while it might be tempting to say, "This doesn't happen in my school," statistics tell a different story. However, the study also suggests that the number of offenses is higher than the number of offenders, meaning that most offenders are repeat offenders. Therefore, schools don't have to root out many adult offenders in order to tackle the problem, only a few, but these few must be dealt with firmly because they leave a lot of destruction and pain in their wake.

The Case of John

John was definitely a repeat offender, although most of his students didn't think of him this way, even the ones who were the target of his groping. John was also arguably one of the most popular teachers at his school. He had been at the school forever, and his students, past and present, sang his praises. For years, nothing negative was said about John. He was The Man. Even John's colleagues didn't say much about him, although many were uncomfortable with his popularity and his obvious need for it. But that didn't mean anything, did it? Also, those who felt uneasy about John had no proof to support their suspicions, so until someone came forward to report bad behavior on his part, John's colleagues didn't have much recourse.

John displayed a couple of characteristics that troubled his colleagues but they weren't traits that necessarily suggested he targeted students in a sexual way. First, John was much more interested in students than he was in adults. He spent time with students when he didn't have to, he preferred their company to that of other adults, and he allied himself with students in any conflict that arose within the community. Students loved John because he "had their back" and he was willing to fight for them and their causes, often to the dismay of the other adults within the community.

Second, John was famous for his charisma. Many teachers have charisma but when charisma is the main feature of an adult's personality, it often spells trouble, which is what John's colleagues sensed about him. John's following among students had a cult-like quality to it, which John fostered, again to the dismay of his colleagues. John made sure he was the most popular teacher in school, and he did so by granting favors to some students and holding out the promise of favors to others. Students felt special when John paid attention to them and, as a result, they were willing to overlook his indiscretions.

Finally, John had access to students individually and off campus, which gave him ample opportunity to grope his female students. John coached the girls' tennis team and during away games and even during practice, with no other adults around, John could get physically close to them without much scrutiny. His charisma masked it all, or rather it protected him from disclosure for a long time.

Eventually, one brave young woman in her twenties, who was working through the emotional trauma she suffered literally at John's hands, spoke up and told her story. Soon former students from all eras of John's tenure came forward with similar tales of sexual misconduct, and it became clear that John was a chronic offender who had been getting away with bad behavior for years.

When John's behavior finally came to light, the questions on everyone's mind were, "Why didn't someone say something sooner? How could this have happened right under our noses?"

John's case illustrates one of the most insidious aspects of this kind of behavior and one of the reasons such behavior often goes unreported: Targeted students often fear they will be ostracized by their peers if they speak out and blow an adult's cover. John was so influential with students—his charisma was so compelling and he wielded so much social power—that, given the nature of the teenage world, his victims feared they would invite trouble by telling the truth and breaking rank with their peers.

They were right. For as many students who spoke out against John's behavior, there were even more who came to his defense, supporting him in his newfound role as victim. The students that suffered at John's hand were accused of lying and summarily castigated by their classmates. Over the years, John had cultivated many allies and therefore he didn't have to surrender without a fight. His influence over students continued to cause harm within the community long after his departure.

The good news is the vast majority of adults who work in schools don't behave the way John did. For most adults, "don't have sex with students" is a no-brainer. But when it comes to some other behaviors, like touching students in a nonsexual way, things aren't so black and white.

Touching

For the most part, we should avoid touching students in any situation, but this is sort of unrealistic for many of us. Why? Because some of us are just "touchers," if you know what I mean, and our touch is innocuous. Or is it?

The Case of Roberto

Roberto, an English teacher and girls' basketball coach, was an ebullient guy with lots of experience. He worked hard to connect with his students and it paid off: He was well respected and well liked by all of them, or almost all of them. One day after basketball practice, Roberto noticed that Caroline, a sophomore on the JV squad, was upset about something. Roberto asked Caroline to stay after practice, and when he asked her what was wrong, Caroline burst into tears. Without thinking about it, Roberto put his arm around her in an effort to comfort her, but immediately realized he had crossed the line. Caroline tensed up, made a quick excuse about having to meet her mother, and ran out of the gym, leaving Roberto feeling regretful and confused about what had happened.

What Roberto didn't know about Caroline, and what none of us knows about our students for sure, is what touch means to them. As a result, it's not enough for us to be clear about our own intentions when we touch students, we must also understand that students may not recognize our intentions for what they are, regardless of how well meaning. Roberto's motivation for touching Caroline was completely innocent, and certainly it was not sexual, but he never considered how Caroline might interpret his behavior. Caroline had a history of being sexually targeted, and Roberto's touch made her feel violated.

Caroline's personal history aside, she might have interpreted Roberto's touch in any number of ways, all of which would have been valid to her, and this is what we must understand. When an adult is on the proverbial witness stand, each side of the story will be weighed against the other, and it's hard for us to make a good case for touching a teenager unless it's in our job description.

So we should avoid touching our students, if possible. Of course, this is a very gray area; it's obvious that nonsexual touching is a far cry from having sex with students, and therefore the guideline should be open to interpretation. For example, a different student with different life experiences than Caroline might have welcomed Roberto's touch. But Roberto didn't touch another student, he touched Caroline and she did have an issue with it, and that's the problem.

Given that we never know where our students are coming from, a good rule of thumb in determining what's appropriate when it comes to touch is to consider common practice within the school community. Is touching students something adults routinely do? If so, under what circumstances is touching students considered acceptable? Also, if you are a touchy adult, ask yourself if you feel comfortable touching students in front of other adults, and if other adults feel comfortable when you do so. That said, even when we are comfortable with touch that doesn't mean our students are, but it's a place to start as we think about how to behave. In addition, if you are a "toucher," consider how you would justify your behavior to a student's parent (the ultimate witness stand).

Finally, some practices of touch are commonplace and socially acceptable, like shaking hands or patting on the back. We should use our best judgment here, and keep in mind that our behavior with students should be uniform; what we do with one student we should be prepared to do with all students. If you are a coach who likes to pat your athletes on the back, make sure you don't single students out with your behavior, and try to avoid patting bare skin (as when male athletes have their shirts off or when swimmers are in their suits).

Talking with Students about Sex

The same rule of thumb applies when it comes to talking with our students about sex. What's common practice within the community? Some of us in the teenage world are paid to talk with students about sex. School nurses, health teachers, counselors, and biology teachers, even some coaches, all might talk to students about sex during the course of their work. Be that as it may, none of us should talk to students about our own sex lives—that's always inappropriate. The guideline to not talk with students about sex applies to conversations that occur beyond the requirements of the curriculum and/or involve the sharing of personal and intimate details about either the adult's or the student's sex life.

As with the guideline to not touch students, this guideline can be open to interpretation. Let's say a student confesses something personal to us, or shares intimate details without being prompted. How should we deal with this? Or, what if a student talks about sexuality with us in generalities? For example, what if they disclose something to us about their orientation or general dating life? What's appropriate, and where do we draw the line?

Is It My Job?

One way to determine whether a discussion about sex is appropriate is to ask ourselves the question, Is it my job to have this conversation?, Am I getting paid to discuss this?, and Is this part of the curriculum? Another good question is, Is this conversation necessary? If the answer to any question is no, then chances are good you should picture yourself on the witness stand and avoid the discussion altogether.

The Case of Audrey

Audrey needed to imagine herself on the witness stand because she talked to her students about sex all the time, and she wasn't getting paid to do it. Audrey taught Spanish at a boarding school. She also dated a fellow teacher and dispensed information about their intimate lives to her students freely and frequently.

One afternoon, Audrey heard a knock at her dormitory apartment door. Without thinking, she opened the door while still in her bathrobe. A startled student, embarrassed to find Audrey looking disheveled in the middle of the day, mumbled a few awkward words. Audrey blurted out, "What do you want? I was having sex with my boyfriend and I want to get back to it."

Suffice to say, the student didn't have a response.

Audrey's behavior was less harmful to her students than John's was; however, her penchant for self-disclosure crossed a similar boundary. What to Audrey seemed like edgy and mature self-revelation was nothing more than verbal exhibitionism, and it made her students uncomfortable and embarrassed, as much as for her as for themselves. If nothing else, Audrey's disclosures made students dislike her; they thought she was weird, a loser, and they stayed away from her, which is not what she intended.

When adults cross a physical or sexual boundary with students, or when we talk to students in sexually provocative ways, we undermine everyone's safety. Even when such behavior isn't illegal (and of course, much of it is), it is highly unethical. When this boundary is crossed in the teenage world, we all must take responsibility for reestablishing safety and trust with students.

3. Don't Talk about Personal Business with Students

Audrey talked about her very personal business with students. Most of us refrain from this type of self-disclosure, but there are many kinds of personal business beyond the sexual realm that we shouldn't discuss with students. Students are at school to learn, not to learn about our personal lives, and therefore we must do our best to keep students focused on themselves and their work, not on us. This guideline to not discuss personal business helps us maintain a healthy distance from our students, and keeps us on the grown-up side of things in the teenage world.

The Case of Bella

Bella crossed this boundary by sharing her personal business with her students, often without knowing it. Bella was a middle-aged

French teacher who felt at ease with her students. She liked the casual banter they engaged in at the beginning of class, and occasionally she joined in. She reported details about her life and marriage and some of the difficulties she had with her son, who was the same age as her students. Bella felt comfortable with her disclosures; she didn't think they were inappropriate, and because Bella never crossed the line like Audrey did, she didn't see a problem. Any of us might do the same thing, and make a casual comment here and there without thinking or reflecting on what's being said.

Here was one of Bella's mistakes, though, and we should all pay attention. Teenagers *do not* want to know the intimate details of our lives. Even when students shower us with attention and questions, the truth is they don't really want to know about our personal business, and furthermore, they wouldn't know how to deal with it if they did. Teenagers want us to meet their needs and, difficult as this can be at times, this is exactly what we're supposed to do.

The Case of Georgia

Georgia was a new high school history teacher and girls' lacrosse coach and was the object of her students' attention, like many young teachers are. While she liked the affirmation, Georgia wasn't prepared for the scrutiny she got from her students. They constantly asked her questions like, Where did you go to college? What are college parties like? Do you have a boyfriend? Where do you live? What do you think of the other teachers? Whereas Bella offered the details of her life freely to her students, Georgia did not, but she also didn't feel comfortable setting limits all the time either.

For new teachers like Georgia, figuring out how much personal information to disclose can be difficult, and there are no absolute right or wrongs, like there are when it comes to having sex with students. The real challenge in situations like Georgia's is to steer the focus of the conversation away from us and back to our students (or to the lesson plan or the practice or whatever). This is a skill we all must master, not just the young and cool among us, although most of us will find that our students express less interest in our personal lives as we age.

Georgia was at what I call "student peak interest level," and therefore she was forever trying to come up with appropriate responses to teenage questions. She felt comfortable revealing some things, like where she went to college (which was something students could find out for themselves anyway), but less comfortable revealing others, like the details of her experiences at college. She also felt awkward holding a line with her students at times, and with being selective about what she revealed and what she withheld. When her students asked her why she responded to some questions but not others, she didn't have an answer, and that made her feel disingenuous.

Georgia also feared that if she didn't answer some of her students' questions, they wouldn't like her anymore. This wasn't the case, but Georgia didn't know it, and therefore she felt torn. While she knew she shouldn't reveal too much about herself and risk crossing the line, she also didn't feel like she could reveal nothing about herself and risk being perceived as withholding. Georgia wanted her students to stay interested in her but she didn't want to let her guard down, and she didn't know how to accomplish this.

Students Aren't Really Interested in the Details

I return to my earlier point that students aren't really interested in the details of our lives. Georgia's situation may appear to contradict this contention; however, we shall see that it doesn't. Despite all the attention her students paid her, if we look beneath the surface of Georgia's situation another truth emerges, one that supports the thesis that teens are not actually interested in us, regardless of whether they're dealing with a Bella or a Georgia. Georgia learned this lesson after a lacrosse game one day.

As usual after the game, a group of girls surrounded Georgia, and on this day they wanted to hear her opinion of the opposing team's coach, who was someone Georgia knew from college (and whom the girls thought was attractive). Throwing her usual caution aside, Georgia told the girls a story about herself and this other coach, and Georgia was temporarily transported away from the present moment by her memories and thoughts. After a while, Georgia realized she had been caught up in a personal reverie, and when she brought her focus back to her students, she realized she had lost their attention.

Georgia's interchange with her students demonstrates that teenagers are interested in themselves more than in us. Teenagers are interested in us to the degree that we're interested in them, and when Georgia's attention drifted away from her students, their attention drifted away from her. Students don't care about our personal lives if our attention leaves them. This point is worth repeating: *Teenagers aren't really interested in us beyond our interest in them.*

Teenagers want to bask in our attention and when they ask us questions about ourselves it is a way for them to keep the connection between us going, and to paradoxically keep the attention focused on them. When we stray too far off the mark, as Georgia did, we make the important discovery that our students lose interest in us when the attention isn't on them. Even the most fascinating among us, which by teenage standards means those of us who are young or hip or cool, do not hold our students' interest long when we don't keep our interest focused on them.

Self-Revelation without Self-Disclosure

The good news is we don't have to disclose anything personal to our students to be accessible and connected to them. Most teachers want to feel connected to students but many assume that self-disclosure is the best way to do this. Luckily, it's not. Instead, our general attitude and demeanor, not specific self-disclosure, reveal what's most important about us as people.

To this end, students don't need to know anything personal about us to know that we care about them and support their efforts to learn. We can reveal our kindness, integrity, quirkiness, and sense of humor without disclosing a single detail of our private lives. So, those of us who fear that students need to know details of our personal lives to stay interested and connected to us can stop worrying. It doesn't work that way.

Over time, Georgia learned that her students didn't really want to know all about her, they just wanted all of her attention. Once she understood this, she felt much more comfortable setting limits. Every teacher will develop a different technique for doing this; Georgia used humor and deflection. When asked a direct question about college parties, for example, Georgia responded in a light manner, "Are you guys crazy? I'm not telling you anything!" She would also turn the conversation back to her students, with phrases like, "When you're old and have graduated from college yourselves, I'll tell you anything you want to know. For now, though, let's get back to work." Georgia found she could communicate warmth and connection to her students in these simple statements, and that that's all her students really wanted from her anyway.

Things to Consider about Self-Disclosure

Each of us has to decide for ourselves how much personal business to disclose to students. The following are some things to consider during this decision-making process:

1. What are your school's policies and guidelines on self-disclosure, if any? What is accepted practice? If your inclination is to veer beyond standard practice, consider having a conversation with a mentor, supervisor, or the principal or head of school to determine what's acceptable behavior and what's not, and where your personal style fits in.

2. Before you self-disclose, remember that information you share with teenagers enters the public domain, and once it does you are no longer the proprietor of that information; you can't take it back. Also, always assume the information you share will be heard by other adults in the community, including parents. I can give you a money-back guarantee on this one. As a school counselor, I had countless conversations with students and parents that concerned the details of teacher self-disclosure. I can therefore promise you that the information we share with students circulates all over the place.

3. How does disclosing your personal information serve students? Does having this information further their learning goals, if at all?

4. How does sharing this personal information serve you? What is your motivation for disclosing details of your personal life to students? What do you hope to accomplish by sharing these details, and how might you accomplish this without sharing details?

5. What are the advantages of self-disclosure in a specific situation? Are there any disadvantages or risks to students if you *don't* self-disclose?

6. If you disclose vital personal information, consider informing your supervisor. Then, when the information circulates within

the community, your side of the story has already been told and is on record.

7. Imagine yourself on the witness stand. What kind of case can you make for your behavior? How would a jury of your peers view it?

The Case for Self-Disclosure, or Not

I believe there are times when adult self-disclosure can be helpful to students but these times are rare. At best, self-disclosure is a distraction for students or simply a turnoff. At worst, it can disrupt and even destroy the relationship between our students and us. In the few instances I know of where disclosure was helpful, the benefit had as much to do with the adult's attentiveness and caring as anything else, and not with any self-disclosure, per se. Adults who share personal information with students may strike a chord, but that chord can be struck as soundly with compassion and empathy as it can with self-disclosure. So, when in doubt, don't say it.

The Case of Uma

Here is a case in point. Uma had dyslexia, so she had enormous compassion for her students with similar difficulties. As an English teacher, Uma encountered many students who struggled to read and write due to various learning styles, and she was always on the lookout for opportunities to support and encourage these students. By all accounts, she was very successful at identifying and helping students who struggled.

One day after class, Uma was reviewing an essay with her student Nick. Nick had been diagnosed recently with dyslexia, and while he was relieved to know what was wrong with him he was still adjusting to this new piece of information about himself. Uma could relate to what Nick was going through, and she told him so. At first, Nick was surprised at Uma's disclosure. He also was a little unsettled that Uma told him something so personal about herself, and yet it made him feel good to know that someone understood his plight.

While it might appear that Uma's personal experience with dyslexia helped Nick, I would argue that it was her ability to empathize and connect to him that made all the difference. Uma wasn't compassionate because she was dyslexic; the two have nothing to do with one another. Uma was compassionate because that's who she was, but she sometimes mistook her own dyslexia as the source of her authority, which it wasn't. Uma was able to relate to her students quite apart from her own personal experience, despite what she thought. While her dyslexia might have informed her view of herself and her students, she didn't need to share her own story to be helpful and effective with them.

Uma's motivations for helping Nick were laudable and appropriate, and she had much help to offer. But once she talked about herself she took the focus off Nick, where it needed to be. Uma had no intention of taking the focus off her students; she just didn't know that that's what self-disclosure does. Once she realized this and stopped sharing her personal story, Uma became an even more effective supporter of her students, and she helped her students immeasurably.

In the end, self-disclosure is a judgment call, and when you self-disclose, be prepared to be judged.

4. Don't Communicate with Students via Personal Email or Phone, Text or Instant Messaging, Facebook, or at Home

Communicating with students has never been easier or more complicated. The advent of digital technology gives students and teachers access to each other twenty-four hours a day via email, text and instant messaging, and cell phones. But just because we *can* communicate with our students 24/7 doesn't mean we should. Now more than ever, we should be thoughtful about our boundaries in terms of time and access to students, and carefully determine how and when we communicate with students in after-hours situations.

I suggest we contemplate our practice around after-hours communication with students not only because it impinges upon our own time but because such communication relaxes the boundary between us and them, and unless our school specifically mandates this practice, it is usually unnecessary. Getting in touch may be easier than ever before but that doesn't mean it's necessary or helpful.

The following are some suggestions about how to maintain boundaries with students when it comes to communication:

1. Know School Policies: Familiarize yourself with school guidelines about corresponding with students (and parents) after hours. Find out whether you are required to check and answer emails or

voicemails at night or on the weekend. If so, be clear about your responsibility for returning messages. For example, if students write emails at midnight saying they need extensions on their work, must you take this into consideration? Are you allowed to set your own guidelines when it comes to such communication? If so, be very clear about your expectations for student behavior and *put them in writing*. If your school doesn't have specific requirements, make sure your personal policies meet with the approval of a supervisor or principal. Finally, if no policies exist, consider joining forces with your colleagues to set consistent guidelines. Teachers can undermine each other's efforts if their practices are widely divergent.

2. Communication via Home Phone and Cell Phone: Some schools don't publish the home or cell phone numbers of employees; others do, particularly boarding schools. Providing the community access to this kind of information says a lot about school culture and expectations for teacher behavior. There are no rights or wrongs when it comes to this, however, make sure you understand your school policies and follow them. If your school doesn't make such information public and does not expect you to be in touch with students after hours, think carefully before you give students access to this information; to do so widens the scope of your role and may increase your liability.

3. Communication via Personal Email: Never communicate with students via personal email accounts. Doing so is problematic for a number of reasons. First, it suggests a level of familiarity and lack of professionalism that is unadvisable. Second, it signals a degree of accessibility that goes beyond the teacher-student relationship, and certainly beyond the time boundaries of the school day and year. There is no school business that can't be handled on a work email account, so stick to that.

4. Communication via Text and Instant Messages: Do not text message or instant message (IM) students unless you are required to do so. Like personal emailing, this type of communication invites a degree of familiarity that is neither advisable nor in students' best interests. Texting and IMing feed the monster of instant gratification. Learning impulse control is an essential part of adolescence,

and these methods of communication don't serve that end. It's fine for teenagers to communicate with their peers this way, but not with their teachers. The student-teacher relationship is and should be different, and therefore it should be conducted via different modes of communication.

5. Communication Online (via Facebook, MySpace, etc.): Many students have personal websites or online profiles. Many adults do too, which puts our students and us in the same virtual online communities without the benefit of the boundaries that exist in real-world school communities. Adults with personal information online should assume students have access to this information. For younger teachers, this might not seem like a big deal; teachers who came of age with this kind of technology do not have the same thoughts about privacy that older teachers do. Regardless of age, though, adults should understand that students don't see us as being separate from our role as teachers, so it's never helpful for students to know too much about our personal lives.

6. Communication at Home: Except at boarding schools, where students meet with teachers in their homes routinely, we should be cautious about conducting any school business, like tutoring, within our homes. We should be extremely cautious about conducting any nonschool business with students from our homes. There are exceptions to this guideline, of course—for instance, when we are friends with a student's family—but, by and large, students should not be in teachers' homes unless required by the school. If this happens, teachers should let a supervisor or principal know what's going on. Also, before inviting students into our homes, we should ask ourselves whether we would invite *all* students into our home. If the answer is no, then chances are the invitation is not advisable and should be reconsidered.

All of the above suggestions aim to help us establish and maintain reasonable boundaries between our students and us, and between our professional and private lives. When we maintain these boundaries and communicate with students in a manner that is consistent with the expectations of the school culture, we reinforce our role as grown-ups in the teenage world.

The Case of Cameron

Cameron, an experienced social studies teacher, came up against a literal boundary with his students. Cameron lived in the same neighborhood as some of his students, as many teachers do. His students knew where he lived and occasionally knocked on his door as they walked by his house. Cameron always felt uncertain about what to do when this happened and, once, his uncertainty led him to invite students inside, where he offered them a drink of water. Cameron quickly knew he had made a mistake when his students, once indoors, commented on his photographs, books, furniture, CD collection—just about everything. Cameron felt overwhelmed by this scrutiny, and vowed never to react to a spontaneous visit by students in the same way again.

Cameron's situation is fairly benign, which is why I use it to illustrate the point about boundaries and communication with students. Cameron did nothing egregious by letting his students into his home for a drink of water but his gesture left a mark. First, it established a precedent, which was awkward for Cameron to reverse. Second, when news of the students' visit got out, it made Cameron look like he was playing favorites, which was not his intention. Were Cameron to deny another group of students entrance to his home, he would have a lot of explaining to do, and therefore he might have trouble refusing the request. And this is exactly what happened. When another group showed up, expecting to be invited in, they challenged Cameron and it made everyone uncomfortable, and his behavior confused his students when he held his ground.

In Cameron's situation, a literal boundary was breached. In cases that involve communication with students via the use of personal email, phones, and Internet accounts, virtual boundaries are breached. Cameron learned two important things from his experience. First, that his knee-jerk reaction to invite his students inside cost him in the long run, and second, that he could be just as hospitable and friendly in his communication with students without crossing a line. The next time students came to his door, he offered them glasses of water without offering them entrance to his home. While he had to hold his ground with this new precedent, Cameron communicated his willingness to engage with his students without crossing an important boundary.

5. Don't Lend or Borrow Personal Things from Students

Material transactions between adults and teenagers in schools should be limited to what the curriculum calls for. When adults and teens lend and borrow from each other, relationships get complicated. We should therefore be cautious about what we give to students and, if possible, we should never borrow things from students. I'm not talking about little things, like pencils. I'm referring to the exchange of personal or valuable items that are not directly related to our work, and whose exchange might serve to change the relationship between our students and us.

For example, we should never exchange money with students unless the practice is directly related to a school activity, like the proverbial bake sale, or is connected to the curriculum in some way. While there are situations in which it is conceivable and appropriate that students in financial need would approach teachers, there are almost no situations in which it is appropriate for us to turn to students for money. So just don't do it. If and when we do spend money on students, we should keep the receipts and get reimbursed by the school. Reimbursement is a good guideline to follow in these situations: When the expense is reimbursable, then the practice is probably acceptable.

When students need money and express this need, we should assess the situation thoughtfully. Is the request a lighthearted plea to purchase a soda from the vending machine, or a more serious request to meet an immediate and essential need, like bus money for the trip home? Obviously, these are very different kinds of requests. The first kind should be refused categorically, but the second kind should be considered carefully.

When a student's safety is at issue or when a basic need is at stake, like getting home from school, and when money is the issue, we must respond. This doesn't necessarily mean, however, that we should use our own money to deal with the situation, but rather it means we must figure out a solution to the problem, one that meets the student's need and maintains an appropriate boundary at the same time. An appropriate first step is to confer with an administrator, and possibly hand over the problem to him or her. In lieu of administrative support, another option is to confer with the business office or the school's financial officer to see whether money is available for such requests. If possible, we should never respond to these requests in haste.

The Case of Molly

This is what Molly did and her action had unexpected consequences. Molly was at her desk grading papers at the end of the school day when Finbar, a student in her geometry class, dropped by and told Molly he lost his wallet and didn't have money to get home. Without thinking, Molly opened her purse and handed Finbar a ten-dollar bill, the smallest denomination she had. Finbar thanked her, said he would pay her back the next day, and left.

The next day, Molly expected Finbar to return the money, but he said nothing. Molly didn't feel comfortable bringing it up, and reasoned to herself that ten dollars wasn't anything to get upset about. When Finbar hadn't paid her back by the next week, Molly decided to say something, and Finbar responded by saying he would definitely get the money to Molly the following day, which he didn't. Molly considered speaking with Finbar again but decided against it. By this point, she realized she had put both of them in an awkward position and she couldn't see her way out of it.

Despite her best efforts, Molly came to distrust Finbar. She knew this was an unreasonable response, but she couldn't help herself. She was angry with him for not abiding by his word, and even angrier with herself for getting herself into this mess and not knowing how to get out. She resolved to never again respond so quickly to such a request.

In order to prevent such dilemmas in the future, Molly did some investigation. First, she asked an administrator if the school had an emergency fund for such requests. It didn't, but Molly's inquiry prompted the school to establish one. Next, Molly made sure she and her colleagues knew how to access this fund for future reference.

Gifts

The exchange of gifts between students and teachers is different than the exchange of money, but it raises some of the same concerns. Many schools place limits on the dollar amount of gifts teachers can accept, particularly from parents.[4] This makes sense for plenty of reasons, not least of which is that it ensures we don't get compromised in our ability to evaluate students fairly. When it comes to presents from students, though, the guidelines aren't usually as clear-cut. We needn't be too concerned about receiving gifts that have no monetary value, like homemade presents, but we should have a policy about accepting gifts that have a price tag attached. That said, even gifts of little monetary value have meaning attached to them, and this is why we need to pay attention.

The Case of Scott

Every morning before class, Scott, a French teacher, enjoyed a cup of coffee in his department office. Scott was a popular teacher, and once his students learned of his caffeine habit, a small group took turns bringing him his morning fix. At first, Scott was touched and flattered by this attention, and because he didn't express anything other than pleasure about his students' behavior, the ritual continued. Scott soon felt uncomfortable about what was happening, though, but the prospect of confronting his students made him anxious, so he didn't say anything and continued to accept the daily offering.

While a daily cup of coffee might not seem like a gift, it is, and such a scenario is loaded with problems. In Scott's case, those problems included creating the impression of favoritism and by extension, exclusion. Although Scott didn't seek out the arrangement, he tacitly approved it, and thereby created a relationship with one group of students that he didn't have with another. Teenagers aren't dumb and the students who didn't bring Scott coffee every morning knew they were not included in a special arrangement, in part because the students who did bring the coffee felt privileged, and it showed.

Scott created another problem by allowing this boundary to be breached, which was that he set up his students to feel obligated to continue the behavior. Because Scott never confronted the practice, some students felt pressure to keep it up, long after it served them to do so. They felt they had to continue or risk a breakdown in their relationship with him. Without ever intending to do so, Scott's behavior gave the impression that he could be bought, and in some ways he could. Our relationship with students should be free of such conditions in order to be effective, which is why we should be very careful when it comes to crossing this particular boundary.

Scott fell into his situation innocently, and this could happen to any of us. When his students brought him coffee, Scott might have nipped the practice in the bud by saying something along the lines of "I appreciate your thoughtfulness, but you don't need to bring me coffee in the morning. You can help me out, though, by getting to class on time!"

This response may sound forced and a little cheesy, but tone is everything, and each of us needs to develop our own style when it comes to articulating boundaries with students. If we respond to students in a way that is direct, kind, and warm they will get the message that we want to stay connected to them, not cut them off. When students offer us gifts, like Scott's did, they are communicating to us that they want our attention. We need to communicate back that they can have our attention just by asking for it, they don't need to give us gifts. Ultimately, the goal of our response to students in these situations is to acknowledge their effort, to be clear about our expectations for their behavior, and to remain connected to them.

6. Don't Spend Time with Students After Hours

We should not spend time with students beyond our contractual obligations to do so. We do lots of things with or for students we aren't obliged to do, like attend school plays or athletic events, and this is par for the course. This guideline addresses our contact with students that is professionally unnecessary and extends beyond these bounds.

I once explained this guideline to a group of boarding school teachers and was met with quizzical stares. At boarding school, where work is life and life is work, it is hard to know what constitutes "after hours." But adults at boarding schools get time off, too, so even they should be mindful of this boundary.

The Case of Brad

Brad was an AP chemistry teacher who often liked to socialize with his favorite students off-campus and during the school day. Brad routinely accompanied students to a mall near campus during his free periods and at lunch, where they drank coffee and chatted. These meetings never involved school business or, when they did, it was a conscious attempt on Brad's part to sanitize his intentions. Brad sought proximity to his students because he was attracted to some of them, and he enjoyed the company of those he wasn't attracted to.

Brad's routine stayed under the radar screen, however, because his behavior was not dissimilar to that of some of his colleagues. At Brad's school, where space was at a premium, teachers sometimes had to meet students off-campus, but always with the purpose of conducting school business.

Brad occasionally saw students on the weekend too, sometimes meeting up with them at athletic events or other school functions and then extending the contact beyond the professional bounds. He sometimes accompanied students to meals or parties, acting like their friend, not like their teacher. Students didn't include Brad in their activities because they sought his companionship or because they particularly liked him. They included him because they knew Brad gave them good grades in exchange for their efforts and that made them feel special.

Crossing this boundary and spending time with students after hours is extremely problematic, and should be avoided at all costs. I can't think of any long-term benefits of this kind of behavior, and the potential hazards are legion. Brad's behavior eventually got him into trouble, not to mention that it caused his students to feel confused and sometimes coerced. Also, those students who were not favored by Brad felt both envy and relief, not to mention a diminished fondness and respect for him.

If we find ourselves in a situation like Brad's, where we're spending all of our free time with students or looking to them to meet our emotional needs, something is amiss and we should seek help immediately. When we observe a colleague struggling in this way, we should also seek help and share our concerns with our colleague and/or a supervisor. Brad needed the intervention of a trusted colleague to extricate him from the situation, and maybe to protect him from himself until he understood the ramifications of his behavior.

7. Don't Consume or Discuss Alcohol or Drugs with Students

Brad didn't drink with his students because he wasn't a drinker, but often he was around students when they were drinking. If it's the case that students are drinking and teachers are around; if teachers are drinking and students are around; or if teachers and students are drinking with each other, something is amiss, at least in the United States. The situation might differ in countries where the drinking age or cultural customs support another practice, but American laws about underage drinking are clear and necessitate a boundary that I trust is self-evident. Perhaps it isn't self-evident, though, because we live in a culture where many parents support underage drinking, either tacitly or directly. We compete against many different forces when it comes to illegal teenage behavior, nevertheless we must recognize our responsibilities and remain steadfast in our practice.

The Case of Jared

Jared was a biology teacher in his thirties who liked to listen to live music on occasion. Jared's musical tastes sometimes overlapped with those of his students, and more than once he ran into students at concerts. Jared liked to smoke marijuana at concerts, and—surprise—so did some of his students, so when their worlds collided at concerts it presented a real problem.

Jared had a couple of ethical dilemmas on his hands when he ran into students at a concert one night when both he and they were in the process of getting stoned. First, he had to deal with the fact that his students knew about his behavior. Second, he had to deal with the fact that he knew about his students' behavior. Jared then wondered whether he should tell someone at school about what had happened, but figured this course of action would impugn his character as much as anything, so he decided against it. He also wondered whether he should talk to his students about what happened, but reasoned this would only confuse the matter. He simply didn't know what to do. In the end, he decided to leave the concert and tell no one.

There are no easy solutions to a situation like Jared's, other than for us to remember that in our students' eyes we are always teachers and role models first. For this reason, we are sometimes held to a higher standard than other adults, which should inform our decisions about personal behavior in public. I don't necessarily believe we *should* be held to a higher standard, but sometimes we are, which is why this guideline is important. As long as we are teachers, we should do our best to stay within the bounds of the law. As far as Jared was concerned, he decided never to smoke marijuana in public again. For him, this was an acceptable restriction to his practice.

8. Don't Talk with Students about Colleagues

Those of us who work in the teenage world are part of Team Grown-Up, and as such it is our job to support our teammates, the other adults at school. One way we can support the team is to avoid talking with students about our colleagues, even when students broach the topic.

The Case of Dominique

Dominique, a middle school social studies and homeroom teacher, relished her rapport with students. She was friendly and accessible, and she prided herself on her ability to relate to kids. Occasionally, Dominique's former students dropped by her classroom to check in and chat, and sometimes the conversation turned to other teachers. One day, two students stopped in and starting complaining about their new homeroom teacher, a woman they clearly didn't like.

The students catalogued their current teacher's failings, and Dominique offered what she thought was support, which is to say she commiserated with their plight. This is exactly what her students wanted to hear, and before Dominique knew what had hit her, the conversation became a bitch session at Dominique's colleague's expense. By the end of the discussion, not only had Dominique listened to her students trashing her colleague; she had also given them the impression that she agreed with them because she hadn't redirected the conversation.

Dominique's collusion in the discussion with her students was made possible by two of Dominique's vulnerabilities, one skill-based and the other personality-based. First, Dominique didn't know how to respond to her students' complaints and so she just allowed them to continue. She literally didn't know how to steer the conversation around without seeming to be unsupportive. Rather than ask the students if they needed her assistance, or if she could help them specifically, Dominique let them complain thinking this was the best course of action, when in fact it was merely the path of least resistance.

Second, despite her success as a teacher, Dominique often felt insecure about herself as a professional, so she was relieved to hear that one of her colleagues wasn't perfect either. The truth was, Dominique allowed the conversation with her students to continue because it made her feel better. She wasn't as interested in hearing about the failings of a fellow teacher as she was about feeling better about herself, and her students' complaints served this end. Many of us share Dominique's vulnerability, and frankly it can be hard to get the kind of recognition we deserve when we spend most of our time with our students. But we need to look elsewhere for reassurance, as Dominique discovered soon after her students left her office.

Dominique's students reported to their peers that Dominique was supportive of their view of the new teacher and this information inevitably trickled into the adult world, kicking Dominique in the metaphoric backside. Dominique got caught in a situation that many of us face, which is what to do with teenage gossip.

When Students Have Problems with Teachers

Dominique's students were just gossiping and blowing off steam, but what if their complaints had been legitimate? Shouldn't we talk with students about our colleagues then? When we hear troubling information about colleagues we shouldn't keep it to ourselves, but we should be prudent about how and with whom we share this information. Ideally, we should share this information with an administrator and we should leave investigation of the facts to them.

When we must conduct an investigation ourselves, I recommend we speak to only one student at a time (given the tendency of such conversations to get inflamed when more than one student is involved), and focus the conversation on information gathering and/or problem solving, not on assigning blame or finger pointing. We should be careful during such discussions to remain neutral and not to share our opinions. We can remain supportive of students without agreeing or siding with them and, until we have the whole story, and even after we have the whole story, we must be careful not to pit ourselves against our colleagues.

As adults who work in the teenage world soon discover, talking with students about other adults is tricky business. We must be prudent when we find ourselves in this situation, and under no circumstances should we initiate such conversations unless what we have to say about our colleagues is both positive and professional. Dominique might have shifted the course of her conversation with her students by saying something like, "You sound pretty frustrated. Is this something serious, or are you just venting? If it's serious, then let's figure out how I can help you.

If it's not serious, then let's not talk about Mrs. X anymore. Perhaps you can tell me about some of the other stuff that's going on with you. I'd really like to hear about . . ."

9. Don't Keep Student Secrets

In a sense, Dominique was keeping secrets when she allowed her students to complain about their teacher. Dominique also gave her students the impression that she was interested in their gossip because she didn't help them define a specific problem (and there wasn't one, really), and because she didn't redirect the conversation. Had she invited her students to identify an actual problem, rather than allowing them just to complain, Dominique would have communicated something entirely different, and she wouldn't have led them to believe that she agreed with their complaints, something she never intended to convey.

Students often want to confide in us, just as Dominique's students did, and many such confessions are harmless. But some are not, and therefore we must be careful not to agree to keep students' secrets or make promises to do so.

Dominique Again

Let's return to Dominique. One day, Becky, a homeroom student, came to Dominique in tears. Becky was very upset and it took Dominique a while to calm her down. Once Becky stopped crying, Dominique asked her what was wrong. Becky started to tear up again and asked, "Can you keep a secret?" Dominique, caught up in Becky's emotional plea, told her that, yes, she could keep her secret.

Becky told Dominique she had just witnessed a fellow student cutting her arms with a razor blade in the girls' bathroom. Becky described a pretty graphic scene, and immediately Dominique knew she had to respond to the situation and thus break her promise. When Dominique explained this to Becky, Becky became agitated and angry. Becky pleaded with Dominique, arguing that she was the only other student in the bathroom and that the student who was cutting would know Becky had tattled on her.

Fortunately, Dominique understood her responsibility in the situation. She began by assuring Becky that she wasn't tattling, and that she had done the right thing by telling an adult what was going on. She told Becky that it was her, Dominique's, responsibility to get help for the student in the bathroom, and that she was going to do that now. She also led Becky to the nurse's office, where Becky could calm down and where Dominique could consult with her colleague about how to proceed. When they arrived at the nurse's, Dominique thanked Becky for being courageous and for doing the right thing, and she told her she would check in with her later to make sure she was okay.

Students often confuse their desire for safety and compassion with a request for confidentiality and, as a result, they ask us to keep secrets when what they really want is our support or help. We should keep this in mind when a student asks us to keep a secret. When this happens, we should attempt to see beyond the request and determine how to help them without agreeing to keep their secrets.

When we make a mistake, though, we should acknowledge it as soon as possible (if not directly, then by way of explaining what we must do to deal with the situation, as Dominique did), and usually students will respond well. Students know we're in charge and they know we are responsible for helping them when they're in trouble. When they share volatile information with us, as Becky did with Dominique, they understand on some level that we can't keep their secret, which is why they confide in us in the first place. Becky needed Dominique to take charge of the situation, but Becky didn't want to feel like a gossip or snitch, which is why she asked for Dominique to keep her secret in the first place. Luckily, Dominique didn't keep Becky's secret. Instead, she executed her duty to keep her students safe, and she made sure both students got the help they needed.

10. Don't Go Beyond the Scope of Your Role

Dominique couldn't help her students by herself, however; she needed some assistance. Dominique was not a school nurse or a mental health counselor, and given Becky's description of the problem, one or both of these people needed to intervene in the situation. In this case, Dominique consulted with the nurse and the counselor and let them deal with the student in question. Had Dominique decided to go it alone, she would have extended herself beyond the scope of her role and could have made the situation worse. This guideline to stay within the scope of our roles is for situations like Dominique's, and it serves to protect our students, our schools, and us.

The Case of Brian

Brian was a math teacher who often conversed with parents in his capacity as student advisor. Brian felt it was part of his job to listen to parents' complaints and, because he was a good listener, sometimes he heard about their private woes. During one such conversation, Brian suspected the mother of one his students was depressed. When he questioned her about her mood, the woman agreed she felt down, at which point Brian suggested she seek help.

Had Brian stopped there, things would have been fine. But he took things a step further, and recommended names of doctors and specific counseling centers to his student's parent. Brian's wife was a psychiatrist and he knew a lot about counseling, and because he knew a lot, he assumed he should share this knowledge with this parent. But even if he had been a psychiatrist himself, it wasn't Brian's place to give advice in this situation. In this conversation, Brian was serving in his capacity as a teacher, not as a doctor, and he needed to stick to his prescribed role. We get ourselves in trouble when we go beyond the limits of our roles, even when it seems like a reasonable thing to do, as it did to Brian at the time.

Because we are in positions of authority as teachers, people sometimes think we should know everything, and that we should have answers to every problem. Brian was tempted to go beyond his role as teacher because the parent he dealt with was very vocal about her problems, and because she looked to Brian for help. Brian wanted to be helpful, as we all would in this situation, and so he shared what he knew; however, what he shared extended him beyond the bounds of his expertise. Brian understood his error when his principal explained to him that by dispensing such advice he had placed himself, the school, and the parent at risk.

The next time a parent asked for advice, Brian knew not to extend himself so far. Instead, he suggested the parent call the school nurse or a senior administrator for guidance. Initially, Brian feared that if he didn't have an answer to a problem he wouldn't be doing his job, but over time he realized that he could be just as effective by making the appropriate in-house referral. In fact, Brian found that by sticking to his role as teacher he could be much more effective in his work. By sticking to his area of expertise, Brian felt more confident and competent as a result, and he no longer felt like he needed to have the answers to everyone's problems.

It is our job to stick to our roles and execute them well and we should feel confident that this is enough.

DO'S

The following do's are five things adults should do to support healthy relationships among each other and outside of the teenage world.

1. Do Understand and Follow School Policies, Procedures, and Best Practices

This guideline is as straightforward as it gets. We should make sure we understand what our community expects from us and abide by the rules. Playing by the rules is the best way to maintain appropriate relationships with our students, and it's also a great way to support other adults. When we follow the rules, we ensure that our community remains healthy and strong.

The Case of James

James, an English teacher, took a pretty relaxed approach to his school's policy about punctuality, and so he arrived late to class on a regular basis. Even when his department head reprimanded him for his tardiness, James continued to arrive to class five, ten, or even fifteen minutes late. Needless to say, most of James's students loved his casual attitude about attendance, and most of them took advantage of James's laissez-faire attitude by being late themselves. What James didn't anticipate, though, was that his behavior had repercussions beyond his classroom, and that his attitude affected lots of people, not just the students in his class.

For instance, on more than one occasion other teachers had to deal with James's students when they roamed the halls before James arrived to class. This did not endear James to his colleagues, nor did they like it when their students grumbled when they started their classes on time. James's neglectful attitude set a precedent, and some students wanted all their teachers to be as lax with them as James was.

Following the rules is how we pledge our allegiance to our school community, and it is essential to our success in our work. The grown-up community is our most important ally in our work in schools, and without it, we have difficulty keeping our relationships with students healthy and manageable. When James finally got the message that his behavior was not acceptable, everyone was better for it.

2. Do Seek Assistance When You Need Help

All of us can get caught up in the frenzy of the teenage world at some point, and we all make mistakes. There are no exceptions. We should therefore seek help when we face challenges in our relationships with teenagers. This means we should identify people within our community whom we trust and who can assist us, and confide in them when problems arise. Hopefully, one of these people will be a senior administrator: the principal, assistant principal, dean of faculty, or department chair. If none of these people seems appropriate, then we should confide in a trusted colleague. But we must confide in someone. We should talk about what's going on, get someone else's perspective on the situation, and get help if necessary. We should never act like cowboys and go it alone.

The Case of Cole

This is what happened to Cole and it backfired. Cole tried everything to settle down his physics class. Nothing worked. As his students got more out of control, so did he, and finally he lost his temper and left the classroom, slamming the door behind him. He went to the faculty room to calm down but told no one what had happened. But a student did, and the next morning Cole was called into the principal's office to explain his behavior. Had Cole told someone about the situation immediately, chances are good he would have had assistance and guidance from Team Grown-Up. As it was, he now had to explain his behavior *and* defend himself, which made the situation worse.

Warning Signs

The following are some warning signs we should heed when it comes to our experience in the teenage world, and we should seek help immediately when one of these signs arises.

Feelings of Loneliness or Isolation. We should reach out immediately when we start to feel lonely or isolated in our work. This is more of a challenge for introverts, like Cole, but we should do it regardless of how awkward or uncomfortable it feels. When we feel lonely or isolated, we are at greater risk for looking to students for support and cutting ourselves off further from the adult community.

Feelings of Frustration or Anger. We should also seek help when we feel frustrated or angry, and certainly if we feel these emotions for extended periods of time. Dealing with teenagers can be crazy making, so we must make sure we don't harbor these feelings for long. Frustration and anger generally indicate we need to process what's happening in our work, and that we could benefit from the support and counsel of someone who can commiserate with us and help us see through the mire. This is what Cole needed, and a consultation with colleagues probably would have helped him resolve his situation quickly.

Unanswered Questions. We should be wary of thinking we must have all the answers, especially when it comes to dealing with teenagers. No one has all the answers, which is why we should work together to help each other with our challenges. When we have questions about a particular situation, or about teenage psychology, or boundaries—anything—we should seek help. This is what we advise our students to do when they don't have all the answers, and we should expect nothing less of ourselves.

The Need to Confess. When we've done something that doesn't sit right with our conscience, we should talk about it; we should confess. I use the term *confess* loosely here, and I don't mean to suggest that teachers should feel duty-bound to share every fleeting thought or action with their colleagues. I do believe, however, that there are times when we hold information we shouldn't, and when this happens we should unburden ourselves to a trusted colleague or administrator. Our need to confess indicates we need some help with something, so we should seek it out promptly.

3. Do Develop Strong Ties with Colleagues

One of Cole's challenges was that he didn't have strong ties with any of his colleagues. He was introverted and quiet and he liked to keep to himself. He liked a number of his colleagues, though he just didn't seek them out, but he soon realized how much he needed their support when things got messy in the teenage world.

Teachers are the best support for other teachers when it comes to dealing with teenagers. All of Cole's colleagues could have commiserated with his situation if he'd let them, and some of them would have been able to help him brush off the dirt and get back on the horse. Cole would have felt much less isolated and ashamed about his behavior if he'd discussed it with his comrades, and discussing it would have quickly led to a solution.

It's unrealistic to think we can be close to all our colleagues but we can establish strong working relationships with most of them. We should aim to be friendly with all adults within the community, and we should consider all colleagues our allies. This may not be easy to do at times, but it is the best way for us to help ourselves deal with the pressures and challenges of our work. When we feel as though we exist in a community, one in which all adults help each other, we reduce our load exponentially and everyone is happier and healthier for it.

4. Do Support the Grown-Up Team

This *do* is closely related to the previous one. Giving and seeking help is what it means to support the Grown-Up Team. Without a doubt, someone would have lent Cole a helping hand if he'd sought help. Most of us are more than willing to help a colleague in times of need. This supportive attitude strengthens schools and makes our work more satisfying.

We must remember that we're members of the Grown-Up Team first, even when we dislike or disagree with our colleagues or with school politics. Even a rogue teacher is a member of the Grown-Up Team and trouble is just around the corner if we forget this. Dealing with teenagers takes patience and the aid of the community. We must therefore seek and lend support whenever it is needed, and to whomever is in need. Such an attitude of professional hospitality serves everyone, and it boosts the effectiveness of everyone in the teenage world.

5. Do Get a Life

Work is only one aspect of life, but sometimes the teenage world and our relationships with teenagers overwhelm us and make us think otherwise. It is our responsibility to cultivate a meaningful life outside of work, even when we feel like we don't have the time or energy to do so. In fact, it's precisely when we don't feel like we have time or energy that we most need a life outside work. Outside attachments and interests give us perspective and make us better teachers.

So, just get a life: Take a break. Go to the movies. Play an instrument. Exercise. Fall in love. Raise a family. Get a hobby. Listen to music. Sing in a choir. Join a team. Volunteer. Play with your kids. Rake the leaves. Sleep in on the weekend. Run with your dog. Read a book. Talk to a friend. Write some poetry. Build some furniture. Participate in local politics. Read the paper. Watch the sunset. Turn off the computer. Write a letter. Travel in the summer. Eat a great meal. Take a risk. Forget about work.

Get a life!

EXERCISES AND REFLECTIONS

1. Which of the don'ts are easy for you maintain and why? Which are not and why?
2. Consider a time when you transgressed boundaries of one of the don'ts. What happened? How did you resolve the situation? What kind of support did you seek, if any, in the aftermath of the incident(s)?
3. Consider a time when a colleague transgressed a don't boundary. How did you discover this transgression? How was the situation resolved, and did you play a part in resolving the situation? If not, how might you have assisted your colleague, the student, or your school in resolving the situation?
4. Are there any school guidelines you don't agree with? If so, why? Would you add any guidelines to the list, and if so, what

are they? What is your rationale for your additions, and how do your additions serve to maintain boundaries between adults and teenagers?

5. Are any of the do's and don'ts transgressed regularly in your school community? Are there any guidelines in your community that are missing from this list, and if so, what are they and how do they serve your community?

6. Discuss the do's and don'ts with some colleagues and prioritize the list, from most to least important. Which are the most important for your community and why? Which are the least important and why?

7. What is the process for dealing with transgressions at your school? How do you think adult transgressions should be dealt with? What consequences should adults receive when they violate boundaries and who in your community should deal with adults in these situations?

8. Consider the case of Jared, who ran into his students at a concert. How do you think Jared should have responded? What would you have done if you'd run into Jared at the concert?

9. Who are the colleagues you like, trust, and feel close to professionally or personally? Consider a time you sought support from a colleague. Why did you seek support? How did your colleague respond? Consider a time when a colleague sought your help. What happened and how did you support your colleague?

10. How do you cultivate a life for yourself outside work? What activities do you engage in to get your mind off work? How would you rate your ability to put your work aside and enjoy other things? How would your partner/spouse, family, or friends rate your ability to put your work aside?

CHAPTER SUMMARY

There are a few key behavioral guidelines adults should follow in the teenage world to make sure that the boundaries between students and adults remain strong and well articulated. The do's and don'ts in this chapter cover aspects of our relationships with our students and with each other, and when we follow all of them, we support a healthy school community. It is our job to make sure we understand the limits in our relationships with students, and work to keep our relationships with our colleagues strong.

NOTES

1. Laws about confidentiality vary from state to state, and laws pertaining to minors vary depending on the age of the child. For instance, school personnel may have to report what is told to them by a twelve-year-old where they might not have to report the confessions of a seventeen-year-old. All adults employed in schools should be aware of the laws in their state and school district and follow the prescribed mandates.

2. U.S. Department of Education, Office of the Under Secretary, *Educator Sexual Misconduct: A Synthesis of Existing Literature*, Washington, D.C., 2004.

3. Ibid, p. 22.

4. Some schools have gone to great lengths to prevent parents from lavishing gifts on their children's teachers. While teachers might welcome such attention by parents in the short run, in most cases teachers soon realize that expensive or valuable gifts come with a heavy price. For example, one teacher received a beautiful and valuable antique fabric from the parents of an underachieving 10th grade boy. At first, the teacher felt pleased and flattered, but these sentiments soon turned to frustration when she realized these parents now expected her to deal with the motivational and disciplinary issues that they were unwilling to tackle with their son. After accepting the gift, the teacher felt hesitant about discussing with the parents their relationship with their son and the expectations the school had for the parents to help their son achieve in school.

6

FIVE GUIDELINES FOR ADMINISTRATORS: THE A-TEAM

Administrators are ultimately responsible for the health of the school community and for the behavior of the adults who work with teenagers. Administrators should work in teams to manage the phenomenon of adolescence and to help adults in the community understand how the teenage brain operates. There are five guidelines to help administrative teams with this task: assistance, transparency, education, assessment, and management. Together they form the A-TEAM, and they serve as a framework for thinking about and managing adults in the teenage world.

HELPING ADULTS IN THE TEENAGE WORLD

Everyone who works in the teenage world faces challenges in their relationships with teenagers, and ultimately administrators are responsible for helping adults deal with these challenges. Some challenges are serious while others are not so serious, but we should acknowledge and deal with all of them in some manner, regardless of degree. When we don't deal with them, or when our mistakes are repeated or egregious, all of us in the school community are vulnerable, especially administrators.

Throughout this chapter, I address some of the issues administrators must deal with in their role as supervisors of adults in the teenage world, and provide guidelines to increase adult resilience and reduce administrator vulnerability to the viral aspects of adolescence. This chapter can help anyone who works with teens but especially those administrators who set the course for the entire school community and who have jurisdiction over adults who work with students. This group includes principals and heads of school, deans of faculty, vice or assistant principals, division heads, and so on. Administrative titles and responsibilities vary from school to school but, specifics aside, most administrators are in the business of helping adults deal with teenagers, and this chapter is for them.

THE FIVE GUIDELINES: THE A-TEAM

The five guidelines that support administrators in their role as supervisors of adults in the teenage world are: (1) Assistance, (2) Transparency, (3) Education, (4) Assessment, and (5) Management. Together they form the A-TEAM. This acronym suggests that administrative work is about teamwork and that administrative teams lead the way in schools. Thus, the A-TEAM is a set of guidelines *and* an actual team of people that uses these guidelines to help adults manage their relationships with teenagers and practice grown-up skills in schools.

In the previous chapter, I outlined specific do's and don'ts adults should practice in their work with teenagers. In this chapter, I stay away from absolutes because I believe almost every situation that involves adults, teenagers, and the fever of adolescence is complicated from an administrative standpoint, and often problems that occur between adults and teenagers have multiple solutions. In addition, these solutions may not be obvious except in cases of illegality or extreme negligence. Therefore, in lieu of do's and don'ts, I offer guidelines to help administrators think critically about their work managing the phenomenon of adolescence and the adults who work in the teenage world.

Guideline 1: Assistance

The first guideline for administrators is *Assistance*, which means giving help and getting help whenever possible. The teenage world is a complicated place, and leading a community of adolescents should not be attempted in isolation. Administrators need more support than any other adults within a school community, and therefore the A-TEAM starts with assistance.

The truth is being an administrator is a lonely job. Experienced administrators understand this. They recognize that nobody within the school community cares about their problems. In this way, being an administrator is sort of like being a parent: It is a thankless role with lots of responsibility and very little glory. Fortunate administrators have one or two people with whom they share responsibility, just like parents do; unfortunate ones go it alone. Given this reality, the first guideline for administrators who work in the teenage world *must* be assistance. Without it, the job is even harder than it needs to be.

The Polarizing Nature of Adolescence

One of the reasons administrators need assistance is because the phenomenon of adolescence often polarizes the community when it infects adults, and this can affect how the entire school functions. How does this happen? Well, teenagers frequently experience the world in black and white and therefore their thoughts and feelings can be extreme. Teenagers live in a world that teeters between good and bad, heroic and villainous, victimized and perpetrating—all day long. Adults often get pulled into this world of extremes because teenagers project their inner worlds onto the outer landscape, and adults are part of that landscape. As a result, adults are cast as players in the teenage drama simply by doing their jobs, and often they get pitted against one another inadvertently in the process. This is polarization, or splitting.

Adults, then, can be the bad guys or the villains in the teenage drama, but they also can be the good guys. This can split the community, for instance when teachers are good guys and administrators are bad guys. Even when the fever of adolescence is high and teenagers are behaving at their worst, it can be difficult for adults to see how they're being affected by what's happening. The phenomenon of adolescence reveals itself sometimes only when symptoms arise, like when communities become polarized, for example, by which point it's hard for adults to extract themselves from the drama. This is when administrative expertise is crucial. Administrators must help adults see what's happening beneath the surface of the teenage play and return the community to a healthy equilibrium.

This may be the biggest challenge administrators face when it comes to dealing with teenagers and the adults who work with them. Administrators must understand the dynamics of adolescence and help teachers make sense of what's going on when they get carried away. This is almost impossible to do in isolation precisely because much of adolescent behavior is unconscious, therefore administrators must assist each other in making sense of what's happening if they hope to avoid getting carried away by it themselves. Without assistance, administrators can get caught up in the same frenzy that other adults do, and when this happens, the whole community is at risk.

A-TEAM Membership

The A-TEAM's job is to provide members with support and guidance with issues related to adolescent psychology and development, or with the viral nature of adolescence. The A-TEAM should be comprised primarily of administrators and select faculty, and ideally it should have a core group of permanent members, although it's helpful to keep an open mind about membership. In the long run, it's important to balance stability with flexibility to ensure a healthy group dynamic.

The A-TEAM should also include at least one person who has expertise in adolescent psychology and school systems. It's not enough to have an expert in just one of these fields. It's important that the A-TEAM gets perspective from someone who understands both adolescence *and* schools, and thus how adolescents behave *in* schools. This might be the school nurse, counselor, or someone else with similar expertise. This person does not necessarily have to be member of the school community. Outsiders can lend invaluable support when the adolescent bug affects the whole community, if for no other reason than they can lend perspective. Administrators should therefore consider retaining an outside consultant as a permanent member of the A-TEAM, or for those times when the adolescent infection runs wild.

In addition, it's important to include the parent perspective on the A-TEAM, although this doesn't mean parents themselves should be included on the team. When the phenomenon of adolescence is in full force, it affects parents too, and this means schools sometimes deal with fallout from the parent community. Anticipating parental reaction helps administrators manage this constituency effectively. In my experience, parents are extremely grateful when schools acknowledge their perspective in difficult situations that involve their teenage children.

A-TEAM Meeting Schedule

The A-TEAM should meet regularly to discuss issues as they arise, but also to conduct ongoing assessments of all aspects of community functioning. Meeting once per week is probably sufficient, and more frequently and as needed during a crisis. In order to be effective the A-TEAM should not be an ad hoc committee for several reasons. First, the work of the A-TEAM should not be bound to crisis. In order to perform assessments and the other duties needed within the community, the A-TEAM should have a regular and ongoing agenda.

Second, the team needs to function as a group in times of calm to be successful in times of distress; if the team meets only during crisis, a sufficient level of trust and familiarity will not be in place for the effective functioning of the group. Finally, an established meeting time, place, and agenda (all of which can shift, of course) establishes within the community an awareness of and an appreciation for the issues that concern the A-TEAM.

Trust and Honesty

In order to give and receive assistance, administrators should trust one another and develop methods of communication that serve to keep the contagious aspects of adolescence at bay. To this end, administrators should be honest with each other at all times without fear of retribution or hostility, or of hurting one another's feelings, even when such honestly is unpleasant. Good administrators have tough skins without being tough characters, and they recognize the value of feedback and constructive criticism from the A-TEAM.

Importance of Feedback

Effective administrators don't care where they get helpful feedback, only that they get it. They look to sources both above and below them in the chain of command for information and guidance because they feel secure in their positions and roles. When administrators can't do this—when they feel insecure about their position or threatened by others—this indicates that the A-TEAM needs some reinforcement and probably more assistance. In addition, administrators should be prepared to hear feedback that implicates them in any of the problems in their community. The drama of the teenage world affects everyone, including administrators, so when it comes to dealing with problems that involve teenage craziness, administrators should be prepared to discover that they've been affected by this craziness themselves.

Considering the Parallel Curriculum

The most important task for members of the A-TEAM is to help each other understand the demands of the parallel curriculum. The parallel curriculum, you will recall, is the set of skills apart from the academic curriculum that teenagers must learn throughout adolescence in order to grow up. This curriculum exists apart from classroom learning but is inextricably tied to what happens throughout the school day. The parallel curriculum is Adolescent Development 101, and a good A-TEAM must understand the implications of the parallel curriculum in order to effectively deliver the academic curriculum. The A-TEAM must also be cognizant of and appreciate the parallel curriculum for adults in the teenage world. This refers to the practice of the seven grown-up skills, among other things.

The Case of School A

School A was a suburban, coed, 7–12 independent school. The school had a strong administrative team, whose membership included the class deans, division heads, the school's CFO, development director, and leaders of all the school's programs. The team met weekly and worked together to set school policies and manage procedures. School A's administrative team functioned effectively running the day-to-day operations of the school, but it needed something different to manage the situation when a group of School B students was killed in a car crash after attending a party hosted by a School A student.

Frank, the head of School A, received a phone call early one Sunday morning informing him that four students from School B had been killed the night before when their car swerved off the road. As the details of the accident emerged, it became clear that many of the students in the School B crash were close with School A students, and it didn't take long for Frank's phone to start ringing off the hook with calls from all members of his school community. Frank was informed by multiple sources that groups of School A students were gathering at both the site of the crash and at School B. As he gathered details about how the situation was unfolding, Frank knew he needed assistance to handle the situation. He needed the A-TEAM.

Frank's first call was to the school psychologist. Frank told him what had happened and they discussed the many possible responses the school needed to consider to deal with the situation. Frank then called a meeting of the A-TEAM, which included the division heads, all of the administrators who dealt directly with students, the school's public relations director, the psychologist, and the school's health team, a nurse and a physician's assistant. The A-TEAM convened at the school and set about the task of evaluating and managing the situation.

There were many things Frank and the A-TEAM needed to figure out, but the most important was how to manage the brewing hysteria of the student body. The death of a teenager is a tragedy, and when death strikes close to home school communities are presented with a delicate and important task. The A-TEAM needed to determine how to shepherd their community through the next few days and weeks of shock, and then how to help their students make sense of the tragedy as the real work of grieving began. And they needed assistance to do this.

Frank understood almost immediately that the A-TEAM needed to expand its membership in order to deal with a crisis of this magnitude. The team decided to contact a local mental health expert whom the school contracted for just such emergencies. The team recognized that it needed an objective outsider to help them deal with the situation because the tragedy hit so close to home; many adults within the community felt personally affected by the situation and they needed personal assistance. The outside expert, then, could lend support and guidance, and she could also lend credibility and help facilitate meetings with parents. The inclusion of this expert reassured the community that they were not isolated by this event and that they had the best help available to them.

The A-TEAM then consulted with the parent's association to arrange meetings to help parents support their children through the tragedy.

The team also called a full faculty meeting before school reconvened and with the help of the outside expert, they discussed how faculty could support students throughout the first school day. During this meeting, faculty were coached not only on how to support students but also on signs of trouble that needed the attention of the A-TEAM. Subsequent meetings were scheduled with the full faculty at this time, and smaller groups of faculty were asked to report to their division heads and deans throughout the next few days. The team also convened meetings with different constituencies of students, keeping in mind the developmental differences and needs of each age level.

As the aftermath of the tragedy unfolded, the A-TEAM continued to gather data from the community about what it needed. The team members stayed in close touch with each other throughout the first week, and several times the group altered plans or created new ones based on the information it received from the community. They also met in subgroups to discuss particular challenges, and they met with an expanded membership when the situation called for it.

The case of School A provides a good example of how the A-TEAM functions to deal with crisis. But it also provides an example of the critical role assistance plays in managing the teenage world. Throughout the crisis, the A-TEAM continuously evaluated its need for consultation, reconfiguration, and support, and its composition shifted when necessary to meet the needs of the developing situation.

Guideline 2: Transparency

The second guideline for administrators and the A-TEAM is *Transparency*. Administrators should aim for transparency in most aspects of their work as it relates to dealing with teenagers—and the more transparency the better. Transparency is especially important when it comes to communication and, for our purposes, transparency has as much to do with the process of communication as it does with the contents of the communication itself. People are happy when they feel like they're in the loop, or when they understand how the loop works.

This guideline is less about sharing details or vetting decisions than it is about creating a process whereby relevant information is shared with the school community in a predictable manner. Haphazard or inconsistent communication can be the undoing of administrators in the teenage world because teenagers are haphazard and inconsistent themselves. To this end, teenagers and the adults who work with them need clarity and predictability if they are to stay on track, and so transparency is key to administrative effectiveness and success.

Transparency about Grown-Up Behavior

The most important thing administrators should be transparent about with adults is expectations for grown-up behavior. This can be a challenge, though, as many administrators shy away from this difficult topic because adults often resent being told how to behave. As a result, important conversations about grown-up behavior sometimes don't take place; when they don't, confusion ensues and small mistakes morph into large ones as the fever of adolescence spreads.

The following list of questions and tips about grown-up behavior is meant to help administrators consider how to be transparent in their work with adults in the teenage world:

1. What are the accepted norms for grown-up behavior in your community?
2. How are these behaviors codified and communicated to adults?
3. How does the stated code of conduct serve to guide behavior within the adult community? Do adults follow this code?
4. How does the community discuss grown-up behavior? How are transgressions discussed?
5. What are the consequences for transgressions? Who is responsible for meting out consequences?
6. What is your comfort level in dealing with adults and their behavior? If you need help with this aspect of your work, where do you seek support?

Keep in mind that:

7. Expectations about grown-up behavior should be clear.
8. Expectations should be communicated and reinforced each year.
9. Administrators should be able to talk to adults about their behavior with comfort and confidence.

Transparency in Hiring

The hiring process is the best place to establish transparency about expectations for grown-up behavior. This is an opportunity for administrators to determine a candidate's fit for the job and to discuss cultural norms for behavior. This is also the time for administrators to frontload the specifics of their management style. As one principal put it, "I tell new faculty what I expect in the first interview. They can't say they haven't been warned."

In addition, the hiring process is an opportunity for administrators to determine how skilled candidates are at being grown-up. Not everything about someone's character is revealed during an interview, of course, but a lot is, and administrators should consider asking questions that target a candidate's specific attitudes about the teenage world and adolescent development.

For example, it is helpful to give candidates vignettes that involve typical situations in the teenage world, like managing unruly groups of students and other disciplinary issues. Also, administrators should aim to discover how potential employees deal with adolescent resistance, and how they respond to not being liked by teens. Administrators might also consider asking questions that shed light on how well candidates deal with colleagues and whether they ally primarily with students or fellow adults.

In addition, administrators might explore how "teachable" candidates are in regard to these issues, particularly if candidates are young or new to the profession. Finally, administrators should consider asking questions that encourage candidates to reflect on feedback, especially how they respond to giving or receiving negative feedback.

Transparency in Evaluation

The evaluation process is the next obvious place for transparency about grown-up behavior. This is also a good time to mentor adults who are struggling with their roles as grown-ups. If administrators are clear that the issue of grown-up behavior is part of the evaluation process, then adults are more likely to receive feedback and talk about transgressions and challenges without feeling defensive.

Transparency: A Parallel Process

The process of administrative transparency is what I call a parallel process—it runs parallel to a process that teachers employ with students in the teenage world. Teachers must be transparent with their students to some degree. They must be clear and consistent and they must establish and follow through with consequences in order to be effective in their work. Administrators should do the same with teachers. As teachers manage students, so administrators manage teachers in a parallel process of transparency.

I don't mean to suggest that teachers are like teenagers or that administrators should treat teachers like teenagers. Rather, when administrators are clear with teachers about what's expected of them in terms of grown-up behavior, and when these expectations are consistent, this models appropriate behavior and sets the boundaries within which adults conduct their business in schools. This, in turn, models how teachers should deal with their students, which is the parallel process.

The Case of School C

School C was a large, urban public high school with a very dedicated faculty. The faculty and administration enjoyed a good relationship, for the most part, but the relationship was put to the test when one of the school's most popular seniors was expelled for drinking on campus.

Joan, the principal, was informed one Saturday night that a senior had been caught drinking at a school dance. This was the third infraction in a three-strike system for this student, and it was clear to Joan that expulsion was the most appropriate consequence. By her authority as principal, Joan summarily expelled the student. When news of the expulsion reached the faculty on Monday morning, some of them became incensed by what they considered to be a hasty decision on Joan's part. Students, too, joined a rallying cry to protest what they considered to be an unjust decision, and Joan was quickly put on the defensive.

In making her decision, which she saw as *pro forma* given the student's track record, Joan had not considered the bigger picture of the teenage world, and how elements of both the student and the adult populations might get affected by the vacuum created by the loss of a popular student. Students felt stunned and upset that a key figure in their world seemed to disappear overnight, and faculty felt left out of a decision that had reverberations throughout most of the school. Although Joan had acted within the purview of her role, she had not been transparent about her actions, and her lack of transparency created a number of challenges for her.

In an effort to be transparent, Joan might have considered convening a meeting of the A-TEAM when she learned about the student's plight. The purpose of this meeting would not necessarily have been to consult about the student in question, but rather about how to handle the possible reactions the adult and student bodies would have to the student's expulsion.[1] Joan needed assistance to be transparent, and that's where the A-TEAM could have helped her. Again, transparency is not about vetting or seeking approval for decisions. It's about explaining to the community why or how decisions are made (when the sharing of this information is legal, ethical, and appropriate) and about helping the community deal with the consequences of those decisions.

For example, Joan needed help from the A-TEAM to manage the student response to the situation—the students were angry and upset—and she needed to find ways to help faculty feel included and supported in a decision that didn't, in fact, include them (at least not in terms of the actual decision-making process). Faculty members felt left out and they needed help and reassurance to understand that Joan had acted appropriately. Explaining this to them might not have been enough, though. Some faculty just needed the opportunity to air their views. Joan might have considered calling a faculty meeting before expelling the student, or certainly before word of the expulsion leaked out.

Faculty members also were angry that they had to deal with their students' anger, and Joan needed to help them be transparent and appropriate in their dealings with students. She could have helped faculty anticipate the needs of their students, and helped them figure out ways to manage the collective student reaction. This approach would have made faculty feel included and relevant, and it would have helped them feel confident about Joan's process.

Guideline 3: Education

The third guideline for administrators is *Education*. Teachers need to be educated about the teenage world, adolescent psychology and development, and expectations for grown-up behavior, among other topics. Very few teachers understand these things at the beginning of their careers (and sometimes they never do), and yet such an understanding is critical to their success with students. Most teachers learn through trial and error, which is not a very effective way to learn. Administrators can make their own lives and the lives of their employees a lot easier if they dedicate some time to educating the adult community about these essential concepts.

Creating a Conceptual Framework

My purpose in writing this book is to offer a conceptual framework that helps adults understand the dynamics that occur between adults and teenagers in schools. My goal is to help school communities think about these issues critically and to create professional atmospheres that encourage openness, discussion, and compassion. In my experience, school communities are strengthened when adults are given license to discuss this aspect of their work. But adults must be supported by the school administration to this end; this effort must be initiated from the top.

A good place to start this process is with new faculty. Faculty orientation can be the perfect time to introduce newcomers to what the school community expects when it comes to this aspect of the work. It also signals to the community that talking about these issues is essential to the health and functioning of adults. One way to acculturate adults to thinking about their work is to conduct regular seminars for new faculty throughout their first year or two of service. Administrators and veteran faculty can facilitate these seminars to help newcomers figure out their grown-up roles within the community. Faculty seem to learn best when they use their own experiences as a guide, but vignettes and case studies can also be helpful tools for exploration and instruction.

The most important point for administrators to convey to newcomers (and to everyone else) is that the dynamic between adults and teens is complex and that adults inevitably face challenges in their work with teens. When administrators underscore this point—that everyone is challenged—it liberates adults to discuss their work. I believe that using metaphors like the virus of adolescence to describe the relationship between teenagers and adults helps adults identify some of the challenges inherent in this dynamic, and also to understand that solving problems and discussing transgressions should be a routine and expected part of professional development. This conceptual framework encourages adults to discuss their work without feeling overburdened by self-consciousness, guilt, shame, or embarrassment.

Education about Adolescent Development

Administrators should also consider educating adults specifically about adolescent development, including recent developments in brain research and the connection to learning. This can be done in all sorts of ways, from in-service programs to external professional development opportunities. It is in the best interests of everyone working in schools to be conversant with this information, and it's the administrator's responsibility to help adults understand how and why this information is important and how it can serve them in their work.

Guideline 4: Assessment

The fourth guideline for administrators is *Assessment*. Administrators must be able to assess adult behavior and evaluate how adults function in relation to adolescents in the teenage world. While my contention is that all adults make mistakes in their relationships with students due to the unpredictable nature of adolescence, I do not mean to suggest that all adult transgressions should be forgiven on this account. Sometimes adult behavior crosses lines that must never be crossed, and therefore administrators must assess the adults within their communities and clearly define unacceptable behavior.

When It's Not about Adolescence

The phenomenon of adolescence affects everyone in the teenage world, and many adults behave in ways that are regrettable as a result. It is the job of administrators to figure out whether adult transgressions are the result of the fever of adolescence or of something inherent in the adult, and the challenge of assessment lies herein. In some instances, the chaos of adolescence is not the cause of transgressions between adults and students, and it is the responsibility of administrators to determine when this is the case and to respond accordingly.

The following are some adult personality traits that spell trouble in schools. When problems arise with adults who exhibit any of the following traits, chances are good the problems have little to do with the teenage world and everything to do with the adults themselves. That said, adults who possess any of the following characteristics aren't necessarily bad or ineffective teachers, but they are at greater risk than other adults for getting themselves and their schools into trouble when it comes to their relationship with teenagers.

Inflexible and Defensive Adults

Administrators should be wary of adults who are inflexible or defensive in their approach to their work and within the school community. Savvy adults may defend these traits with assertions of personal integrity and high standards but there's a problem when standards can't be challenged. When adults make mistakes and refuse to examine or change their behavior as a result, this is a very big red flag.

Most adults get defensive on occasion, and this is usually fine. But most adults are able to back off from defensive positions when necessary. Adults who don't or can't back down, or who continue to defend their behavior in the face of well-reasoned opposition, are acting like petulant teenagers, and this is not fine. Administrators must therefore be able to assess the difference between positions that are inflexible or defensive and those that are merely strong-willed.

Inflexible and defensive adults are at great risk in their work with teenagers because the virus of adolescence adapts to its host environments. This means that adults must adapt themselves if they are to outrun and survive infection. When adults can't or won't change, they become increasingly susceptible to behaving like teenagers themselves, and they tend to infect others as they leave destruction in their wake. Adults who are inflexible or defensive also tend to be insecure and unimaginative, and these are also liabilities in the teenage world. Ideally, adults who work with teens should be emotionally adept and agile and should not fear challenge or change.

Charismatic Adults

Charisma is another personality trait administrators should be on the lookout for in the adult population. Charisma is a "special magnetic charm or appeal" and a "personal magic of leadership arousing special popular loyalty or enthusiasm for a public figure."[2] As the definition suggests, charisma is not just a personality trait, it is also the effect such a trait has on others. Charisma can be thus understood as a dynamic process that occurs between magnetic adults and teenagers within the school community. Many adults have appealing personalities and this is a huge asset to their work with teenagers. But charisma implies a degree of influence or sway over others that go beyond this threshold, which is why it can be problematic.

Charismatic adults differ from run-of-the-mill congenial adults in that charismatic adults are often invested in or benefit from the influence they have over others, especially teenagers. There are exceptions, of course, but charismatic adults in the teenage world are at high risk for being influenced by teenagers because teenagers *love* charisma. Teenagers *want* to be charmed and magnetized and, consequently, charismatic personalities often galvanize them. This gives adults with charisma tremendous psychological power over their students, which is another reason why this trait can be problematic.

In addition, people with lots of charisma often don't develop other parts of their characters. This means immature charismatic personalities tend to be shallow and one-dimensional, which is a tremendous disadvantage in their work. These adults are at the mercy of teenagers without even knowing it. When they are adored and fixated on by students, undeveloped charismatic adults don't have the psychological wherewithal to maintain boundaries, and in most cases they don't want to. They enjoy the adulation and attention they receive from students, and if charisma is all they have going for them, such attention feels natural.

Charismatic adults who are drawn to work in schools are often psychological adolescents themselves. They become the Peter Pans of the community, the *puers aeternus*, or the eternal boys.[3] Immature charismatic personalities need and court attention from students, and they don't rest until they get it. Administrators can determine the potential for trouble with charismatic personalities by assessing how well such adults integrate into the adult population and function as part of a team. Charismatic adults with well-developed personalities can work alongside their colleagues without using their charisma to exert control, and they can tolerate not being the center of attention. They also can ally with adults against students when necessary and not feel threatened.

It's important to note that there's nothing wrong with charisma per se. Charisma is a wonderful trait, but when charisma is the defining feature of an adult personality, trouble is usually around the corner in the teenage world, and sometimes it is hard to see because of the blinding effect of the charisma itself.

Student-Focused Adults

Charismatic adults with underdeveloped personalities often forge strong ties with students. Rarely do these adults form strong ties with other adults, though, in part because other adults don't have much in common with them. This is another red flag administrators should be on the lookout for: adults who are primarily student-focused.

Adults who are focused mostly on students have little interest in the adult community within schools. They prefer to deal only with students and they display little understanding of the value of the adult community. Student-focused adults generally do not form friendships with colleagues or participate in adult-only activities at school, and they don't volunteer for leadership roles within the adult community. Their sole interest in working in schools is to connect with students, which is another red flag.

I know plenty of good, effective teachers who don't like many of their colleagues and who would prefer to focus solely on teaching. However, these adults recognize the need to participate within the adult community and they don't shirk their responsibilities. Student-focused adults are more extreme than this, and their isolation and immaturity place them at high risk in their work with students. When adults don't value the adult community in schools, they are in effect putting all of their emotional eggs in the student basket, and this can be hazardous. These adults are at much higher risk for committing transgressions than other adults, if for no other reason than they don't get support from colleagues.

Student-focused adults are also at greater risk than other adults for crossing physical boundaries with students. Sexual predators usually fit into this category, although not always. Most student-focused adults do not engage in physical relationships with students, however they often form relationships that have amorphous emotional and psychological boundaries. Such adults tend to be uncommunicative with other adults or secretive about their work, and they are proprietary in their relationships with students. These are important indicators for administrators to pay attention to.

Adults with No Life

Teaching is an all-consuming job, and many adults who work in the teenage world complain of not having a life. This is normal, and when adults complain it's a good sign because it means they want to have a life beyond their work. But some adults don't want a life, or they don't know how to create a life for themselves, and this is a problem.

It can be difficult to assess whether adults have lives outside work, and it is inappropriate for administrators to inquire about this directly. The problem reveals itself over time, however, often when adults spend all their time at work or expect the community to meet their emotional needs. Ironically, or perhaps understandably, such adults may become the backbone of school communities because they give all their attention and energy to their work, and on the surface this seems like a good thing. Usually, though, this "dedication" comes at a price, whether this price is burnout or identification with students or simple neediness.

School communities commonly praise and reward the efforts of adults with no life, which naturally makes the problem worse. What's wrong with sacrificing everything for work? Well, for starters such adults aren't technically sacrificing anything because they've got nothing to give up. Second, they set a bad example for everyone else, and adults who do have lives outside work are sometimes held to impossible standards because of their no-life colleagues. Adults with no life often feel self-righteous satisfaction at their ability to do more, give more, and participate more than others within the community, and this eventually becomes everyone's problem. When it becomes clear that adults use work as a substitute for life, administrators should take heed.

The biggest concern administrators should have about no-life adults is the degree to which such adults look to the school community, and specifically to students, to satisfy their emotional needs. Well-rounded adults get their emotional needs met in various ways and from various sources, and they understand that work is not the place to get most of these needs met. Some of their needs will be met at work, of course, but not all of them, and certainly not intimate emotional needs. Adults who don't get their emotional needs met elsewhere will naturally look to their work to satisfy these needs. This is not surprising—in fact it makes sense—nevertheless this is a huge problem when one's work involves children.

Adults with no life may seek mirroring, intimacy, a sense of reciprocity, and an experience of companionship from students. These adults are at high risk for forming unhealthy attachments to students and to the school itself, which renders them vulnerable and resistant to change. When work is where the heart is, it is difficult for adults to gain perspective. It is hard for anyone to be impartial and disinterested when personal stakes are so high, and yet impartiality and disinterest are critical skills for adults to have in the teenage world. These skills provide some immunity to the workings of the teenage brain, and they help adults to welcome growth and weather necessary change.

When administrators assess that adults don't have lives outside work, it goes without saying that this should not be capitalized on. Administrators should resist the temptation to let such adults work around the clock or do all the dirty work. These adults should be encouraged to carve out time for themselves, or at the very least they should be directed to spend some of their energy on activities that don't involve just students. The more these adults focus their emotional energy on students, the bigger the problem is in the long run, so if nothing else administrators would do well to find roles for them that provide a balance of duties.

The Likelihood of Change

The above-mentioned character traits are difficult to deal with because they are often intractable and therefore impervious to change. Once a charismatic, always a charismatic, as I like to say. When an undeveloped charismatic—or an adult who is defensive or inflexible or student-focused or doesn't have a life—resists change, chances are good they aren't capable of it. At best, these character traits can be shifted over time and with a great deal of effort (not to mention psychotherapy), and administrators must assess whether such an investment is worth it. At worst, these traits rear their ugly heads again and again and create untold problems, leaving administrators feeling frustrated and exhausted.

When any of these red flags appear more than once, or when administrators find themselves dealing with adult mistakes again and again as a result of these traits, they should consider counseling such adults out of the community or not renewing their contracts. Not all adults are suited to work with teenagers, and adults with the above characteristics may be among this group. Removing such adults from the community can be problematic, however, because often their transgressions are not illegal or unethical, they're just about bad judgment. Administrators should keep clear and consistent records that document all conversations, plans of action, follow-through, and so on with problematic adults. If left unchecked, such adults can remain in school communities for years due to the absence of protocols to deal with them or a paper trail that documents behavior.

Adults with these traits hamper everyone's ability to deal with the challenges of working with teens, because these traits leave them with little resistance to the fever of adolescence. The truth is when the fever infects one adult, all adults are affected in one way or another, and so high-risk adults (or low-immunity adults, if you will) place a big burden on the community and make a lot of mess along the way.

So, who has to clean up the mess these adults make in the teenage world? That's right, the lonely administrator. Therefore, it's critical for the A-TEAM to assess how adults function within the community and ensure that adults who work closely with teenagers are healthy and effective. The A-TEAM should discuss its concerns about particular teachers in a confidential manner and consider strategies to support the adult in question. It is not necessary to institute a system to assess every adult, just a protocol to assess problematic situations as they arise. When it becomes clear via this process that an adult is struggling to maintain grown-up behavior, the A-TEAM should monitor the situation closely and make it clear to the adult in question that they have concerns.

The Case of John Revisited

Let's return to the case of John for a moment, the teacher in chapter 5 whose relationships with students was on his colleagues' radar screen for years. Everyone within the adult community had mild reservations about John but nobody expressed their concerns, at least not in a direct way. Even members of the A-TEAM felt uneasy about him and his popularity, but nothing was done. Should the A-TEAM have responded to something as amorphous as uneasiness? The A-TEAM's job was to assess the situation. Is a feeling of uneasiness part of an accurate assessment? Yes and no.

First, a lot of people had a hunch that something was wrong with John, in part because he delighted in his popularity to such a degree. John was a classic undeveloped charismatic personality; that was clear for everyone to see. This fact should have put him on an active radar screen, but of course this information didn't necessarily mean he was crossing a sexual boundary. Nevertheless, it was important information and it formed the beginning of an assessment. The A-TEAM's first step should have been to pay attention, and John's need to be popular and his huge following among students was worth paying attention to.

Second, the school did have some harder information about John, although it had fallen through the cracks because of inattention. The A-TEAM was aware that John often spent time and attention on students that was extraneous to his duties. In his capacity as coach, he often stayed late to coach particular students, and this behavior was noticed by members of the athletic department. He also spent lots of his own money during away matches, and although he sought reimbursement, it was clear that his practice of spending money on his students did not match the behavior of his colleagues.

Of course, these clues do not necessarily spell trouble in all cases, but in John's case they were important pieces of the assessment puzzle, and the A-TEAM might have been able to intervene had they followed up with him on these aspects of his behavior. This is where the A-TEAM must strike a balance, though, and until clear evidence is discovered, it must refrain from judging prematurely. It is the A-TEAM's job to assess, not to jump to conclusions, and in John's case the initial assessment should have been to monitor and continue to assess the high-risk situation.

Situational Risk Factors

There are times when all adults are at risk of being overwhelmed in their work with teenagers. Starting a new job or career, marital difficulties, a death in the family, divorce, and simple loneliness can affect a teacher's ability to do his or her job well. Administrators should be on the lookout for adults who face these situational risk factors, and offer help in the form of mentoring, counseling, time off, or even sabbatical as a means of keeping effective teachers on board. Adults dealing with significant stressors need support and guidance, and at the very least they need to know that someone at work cares about their struggles. Administrators should let adults know how to reach out for help and what resources exist to support them during their times of need.

Guideline 5: Management

The final guideline for administrators is *Management*. Administrators are responsible for managing the school community as a whole and for setting the tone of school culture (and for cleaning up the mess). To this end, administrative management is critical to the development and maintenance of a healthy school environment. This final guideline addresses the management of the teenage world when the infectious aspects of adolescence infect large segments of the population or the school community as a whole.

The Forest and the Trees

Administrators are responsible for understanding and managing the big picture, or the forest, of the teenage world. Teachers and other adult staff are responsible for tending to the particular trees. An administrator's capacity for understanding the big picture is perhaps the single most important skill he or she possesses in dealing with adolescent culture. This skill includes the ability to understand adolescent psychology, the recognition of the psychological rhythms of the school year (for example, seniors sometimes act out as they approach graduation), and the ability to extract meaning from seemingly random teenage and adult behavior. Seeing the forest of the teenage world in this manner allows administrators to assess their school culture and manage it effectively, and to get it back on track when it inevitably goes awry.

The following examples describe what the teenage world looks like when the phenomenon of adolescence reverberates among large portions of the culture. They are the cultural symptoms, if you will, that administrators should look for in the process of managing the community. While I present the following symptoms as separate entities, they often overlap or coexist, and thus they should be understood as conceptual guides to the imbalanced community rather than as actual entities. Unbridled adolescence is messy if nothing else, therefore the following categories are offered as ways to bring some order to the mess caused by widespread contagion.

Culture of Personality

When adult popularity becomes important, or when adults value popularity as much as teenagers do, the community has a problem. Some adults will always be popular with students, but a *culture of personality* goes beyond this. In a culture of personality, the adult culture mimics the teenage one, wherein celebrities are created and select adults are valued in extreme ways. In a culture of personality, specific adults are worshipped and idolized, although they're not necessarily respected. Such adults commonly develop followings of students, and even of parents and other colleagues, and they do nothing to dissuade their followers from keeping them on a pedestal. In fact, such adults cultivate their cult-like followings and resist all attempts to change.

Fissures can emerge within the adult community in cultures of personality, often along popularity lines. Because not everyone can be popular, the phenomenon of extreme popularity necessitates the existence of not-so-popular adults, and this can be very damaging to the adult community. For every star created among the faculty there exists someone who is not a star, and non-star adults lose among the student community while their star colleagues gain, at least when their worth is measured by teenage standards. Categories of inclusion and exclusion, cool and not cool, and favored and not favored pervade the adult community in the culture of personality.

Adults are judged and valued by teenage standards in cultures of personality. It might seem that teenage standards are the only standards in the teenage world but this isn't the case. Teenagers recognize adult standards too. In fact, teenagers tend to judge adults by teenage standards only when adults permit this to happen. Cultures of personality therefore emerge as a direct result of adult behavior, not of teenage standards. Mature adults do not seek or need teenage adulation and they can moderate the effects of popularity as a result. Immature adults can't do this.

Cultures of personality are commonplace in communities that have many needy and charismatic adults on staff. When the number or influence of such adults reaches a critical mass, communities embrace the notions that adults must be popular to be effective; that entertainment value is more important than content value in the classroom and beyond; and that the practice of cultivating and playing favorites is acceptable and essential to adult success. In such cases, adolescent standards pervade the community and adult standards are eclipsed.

Cultures of personality can be challenging to manage because they have an almost cult-like quality to them and it's common knowledge that cults are hard to crack. When adults seek glory in the attention of teenagers, administrators are up against a powerful force. Managing such adults, let alone the damage they leave in their wakes, can be a full-time job, and the amount of time administrators spend managing adult mess should serve as an indication of how compromised the community is.

Culture of Us vs. Them

Popular adults with cult-like followings often create *us vs. them* cultures within the teenage world, where *us* stands for adults and *them* stands for administration. An us vs. them culture is expected in the teenage world, of course, but only between students, or between students and adults, not among the adult community itself. The us vs. them culture should never connote a division among adults themselves; when it does, something's wrong. When adults stand in united or unyielding opposition to one another or the administration, one of two things is going on: the adults are behaving in grown-older ways, or the administration is ineffectual or overwhelmed, or both. In any case, the administration must manage the situation if it hopes to bring the community back into balance.

One way to get the community back on track is to help adults deal with their conflict productively. Effective administrators recognize that conflict has its place within the adult community. In fact, a certain amount of discord is to be expected, given the power differential between administrators and faculty. Faculty and administration may be at odds over things like salary, benefits, schedules, workload; any of these factors can create tension, and this tension is predictable.

Adults should be encouraged to deal with tension and disagreements openly, respectfully, and without fear of recrimination. Communities that deal with conflict in this way are healthy, and trust and respect prevail. Productive conflict inevitably strengthens a community; it doesn't polarize or split it. In fact, it is essential because it reinforces both the adult community and the boundary that exists between the adult and teenage worlds. When conflict is aired and managed effectively, administrators reduce the likelihood that adults will break ranks and create a culture of us vs. them.

When adults don't stand united within the teenage world they create confusion for students and headaches for themselves. The biggest danger in us vs. them cultures occurs when adults join forces against each other or the administration and bring students along for the ride. When oppositional adults include students in their machinations, they not only divide the community, they make it psychologically unsafe for students. Such adult behavior communicates to students that they must take sides, often against adults they trust, and that the workings of the adult community should concern them. Adults who do this to students are as negligent as parents who force their children to choose sides in parental conflict. It's a rotten thing to do to kids, whether at school or at home.

Us vs. them cultures also emerge when there are many student-focused adults in the community. Student-focused adults identify with teenagers, and therefore they identify with typical adolescent struggles, like separation and individuation.[4] Student-focused adults also don't acknowledge an allegiance to the adult community. In extreme cases, they don't even see themselves as adults at all, and therefore they are apt to view teenage struggles as their own, and vice versa. When this confusion about roles prevails, adults join with students in the inevitable clashes that occur in the teenage world. Unfortunately, they not only join in these clashes, they often incite them, and then they devote their energy to fighting losing battles.

It's normal for teenage communities to split and clash, and when this happens adults should help teenagers make sense of the situation; this is their proper role. When adults stop participating from the sidelines and get into the ring, however, they are behaving like teenagers and the healthy functioning of the community is jeopardized.

Culture of Gossip

Gossip is widespread in the teenage world. It is hard to avoid, at least it is hard to avoid student gossip. Adult gossip should be avoided at all cost, on the other hand, but it tends to flourish in communities where adults are student-focused and/or don't have lives of their own. Gossip may also flourish when adults don't feel like their voices are heard by the administration, or that their opinions don't matter.

Adult gossip can have a slippery-slope quality to it, and in many schools there exists among the adult community something I refer to as *gossip creep*. Gossip creep is the predictable increase in gossip that occurs when boundaries around language and sharing information are relaxed or ignored over time. Gossip creep occurs for reasons as benign as boredom, laziness, or inattentiveness on the part of adults; its impetus is rarely malicious. Adults may gossip about students because it's easy, and because students are what adults have in common in the teenage world. Adults may gossip about other adults or their supervisors because it's a way to let off steam or to deal with unacknowledged or persistent frustration.

Gossip is also mindless, for the most part. Gossip is the antithesis of authentic conversation and connection. Adults in schools work hard and they're busy, which means they don't necessarily have time to connect with their colleagues in meaningful ways. Gossip, then, becomes a shortcut to a sense of shared experience, or it replaces shared experience altogether, and when this happens it is an indication that the adult community needs to find more purposeful ways to connect.

Gossip is most destructive when it occurs between adults and students, regardless of the subject. It is a sure sign that teenage standards prevail when this happens, and adults need to understand how damaging such behavior is. At best, it communicates to students that adults enjoy the same petty pleasures that they do. At worst, it communicates that adults can't be trusted.

Administrators should be aware that it takes only one influential and gossiping adult to send the message to students that this is what adults do. The effect of such behavior is an overall reduction in the level of trust for adults within the student community, and it breeds fear in students that they too might become the subject of gossip. Even when adults gossip with students only about other adults, it is extremely destructive, and such behavior undermines all adult efforts to establish trust and safety within the community.

Gossip is commonly used as a tool to support us vs. them cultures and cultures of personalities. Gossip is the communication method of choice for adults who can't connect to students in other ways, and it's what some adults use as a substitute for authenticity in relationships. Adults who engage in gossip incorrectly believe that this form of discourse increases intimacy, but of course it doesn't. Gossip is a barrier to true communication, and therefore cultures of gossip tend to foster connections that are shallow and insubstantial.

One step that administrators can take in dealing with gossip is to make sure they never do it themselves. This sounds obvious but administrators must remember that they set the tone for the entire community. When adults trust that administrators will not gossip, then gossip among faculty will seem unwarranted and out of place. If administrators communicate to faculty that their opinions are important and will be respectfully heard, then most adults will not feel the need to gossip. Some adults will always gossip, of course, but as their numbers reduce, their behavior sticks out within the community, and this is what administrators should aim for. Cultures shift slowly, and one sign that a shift has taken hold is when problematic behavior stands out and is seen as problematic by a majority of adults.

Culture of Capitulation

A *culture of capitulation* exists in the teenage world when discipline is lax or inconsistent and adults don't hold their ground with students. This culture is one in which compromise reigns—but not the good kind of compromise—and everything is up for grabs. Students and their parents can negotiate virtually anything in a culture of capitulation: rules, limits, and boundaries, even grades. Adults don't understand or perform their duties as grown-ups well in this culture, and they take the phrase "student-centered" too literally. As a result, teenagers basically run the show.

Cultures of capitulation arise when adults feel ambivalent about holding the line with teenagers, and when their default position is to befriend teens and credit them with maturity they don't possess. These cultures flourish when adults pay more attention to what teenagers want than to what they need, and when adults expect teens to regulate and manage their own behavior without grown-up guidance.

The reason I call this phenomenon *capitulation* is because teenagers often yearn to be in charge of everything, and they welcome the opportunity to negotiate things on their own terms. This desire is not inherently bad, of course; in fact, it's developmentally appropriate. But when adults confuse the teenage desire to spread their wings with the ability to fly, adults have surrendered their responsibilities, and everyone suffers. Adults must remember that if teenagers could manage themselves on their own they wouldn't need to be in school. But they can't, and so they are in school.

The culture of capitulation, more than the other cultures, is a product of the times. Relationships between teenagers and adults have changed over the past few generations and this is most evident in places where teens and adults exist side by side, namely, in schools. Today's generation of adults working with teens has a much more familiar relationship with teenagers than was common a few decades ago—and this has its advantages—but difficulties arise when this is taken to the extreme. There's nothing wrong with adults and teenagers relating to one another in familiar or informal ways, but it becomes problematic when adults no longer understand their roles with teens and when teens bear more responsibility for themselves than they can handle.

Adults in cultures of capitulation usually have a greater need than other adults to be liked by teenagers. In such cultures, adults prioritize harmony and find the inevitable discord within the teenage world difficult to tolerate. Teenagers need to learn to deal with conflict and aggression, and cultures of capitulation develop when adults can't accept that teenage behavior is sometimes deplorable. These cultures often have codes of conduct that run counter to the developmental ability of most adolescents, and they may prize behavior that is, frankly, impossible for teenagers to meet. Ironically, cultures of capitulation often have the most aggressive anti-bullying, anti-harassment, anti-everything policies precisely because adults don't hold the line in day-to-day matters and don't understand how normal teenagers behave.

Basically, adults within cultures of capitulation do not attend to the developmental needs of teenagers. Instead, they cater to their own need to feel good about themselves, and they indulge their desire for teenagers to appear mature, happy, and to get along with each other at all cost.

Administrators can combat the culture of capitulation by helping adults understand their roles and responsibilities when it comes to student behavior, discipline, and the general tone of the school. Administrators must also help adults deal with parents who might capitalize on adult weakness or inexperience when it comes to dealing with teenagers. For example, administrators should support adults when it comes to grading, classroom management, and other issues that might cause conflict with parents. This doesn't mean administrators should support faculty without question, but they should support faculty in a process of following school guidelines and adhering to school policies.

AN ADMINISTRATOR'S JOB IS NEVER DONE

Administrators have the most complicated and important job in schools, in part because adolescence can be so insidious and unpredictable. Mistakes happen all the time, and when they do the A-TEAM should assist each other, assess the problem, educate the community about what's going on, be transparent about the course of action needed, and manage the situation. This is challenging and never-ending work, but it gets easier once the A-TEAM is in place and the community understands the challenges adults face in their relationships with teenagers. When administrators do their jobs well, teenagers and adults remain healthy, and when problems arise, as they inevitably do, they get identified and resolved quickly.

EXERCISES AND REFLECTIONS

1. Who is on your A-TEAM, and to whom do you turn for support in your work? What do you do if/when you feel isolated?
2. How do you communicate your decisions and your decision-making process with your school community? What kinds of feedback do you get about your style?
3. How well versed is your faculty about adolescent development, their roles as grown-ups, and so on? How would you rate the maturity level of the adults at your school?
4. Consider a time when you had to deal with a problem with a faculty member. What about the adult's personality contributed to the situation, and how did you deal with this? How did the phenomenon of adolescence contribute to the situation, and how did you deal with this?

5. Consider a time when your adult community behaved more like teenagers than like adults. What symptoms did the community have, and how did you identify and deal with them?
6. What is the hardest aspect of your job, and why? Where do you get support for doing this part of your job?
7. What do you like most about working with and supervising adults? What do you like least?

CHAPTER SUMMARY

Administrators must help adults who work with teenagers understand how to manage their relationships with adolescents. Administrators should work together as a team to understand how the school community and individual adults react to the viral aspects of adolescence and keep the entire community healthy when infection pervades the population. The five guidelines for the A-TEAM help administrators manage adults in schools and assist them in thinking creatively about how adolescent psychology manifests within school environments.

NOTES

1. Every school handles discipline differently. At School C, adults handled discipline exclusively (School C did not have a disciplinary committee that included student members, as some schools do), and the principal dealt with situations that involved third strikes or possible expulsion from the school.

2. Merriam-Webster Online Dictionary (2008).

3. Women can be just as immature as men, of course, although more often than not charismatic men gain higher profiles within the teenage world than charismatic women do, at least in coed schools. In my experience, charismatic women who wield psychological sway over students are less common in coed schools because pathological charisma comes down to one thing, power, and in coed communities power is not shared equally by men and women. So, women are more likely to act like Peter Pan (who is quite androgynous, really) in all girls' schools.

4. Part of the parallel curriculum for teenagers during adolescence is separation and individuation. During this phase of development, teens need to discover who they are, independent of their parents and other adult authority figures (i.e., teachers). During this psychological process, teenagers may exhibit oppositional, resistant, or just plain disagreeable behavior as they struggle to figure out who they are. This process is normal and over time, as teens learn who they are and gain confidence in themselves, their need to oppose and resist adults wanes.

7

THE EIGHTFOLD PATH OF ADULT SELF-CARE

The Eightfold Path of Adult Self-Care is a set of practices that helps those of us who work with teenagers attend to our own needs. Self-care is critical because our relationships with adolescents in the teenage world are challenging. It is not enough for us to take care of just our students; we must also care for ourselves if we want to be effective in our work with teenagers.

WHAT THE BUDDHA TAUGHT

The Buddha taught his followers that life is suffering, and that we suffer because we desire. He said that we can ease our suffering, and he offered a set of practices called the Noble Eightfold Path as a method for doing so. These Buddhist teachings are known as the Four Noble Truths, and I believe they have something to offer us in our work with teenagers. Let me explain.

First, the truth is that working with teenagers is challenging. *Suffering* may be too strong a word for it but let's face it, sometimes our work in the teenage world is really hard. Second, another truth is that our work is hard because we desire to do well, we want our work to mean something, and we want to be effective. One way we can be effective is to take care of ourselves, and to this end, I offer an *eightfold path of adult self-care* specifically for those of us who work with teenagers.

I have liberally adapted the major concepts of Buddha's Eightfold Path for this purpose, but by doing so I do not mean to suggest that this method of self-care is philosophical or religious in nature. The Buddhist template merely lends itself well to adaptation. That said, what Buddhism offers beyond adaptation is the notion that self-care and psychological well-being come from intention. We must cultivate healthy habits—they don't just happen—and that's what the Eightfold Path is about.

THE EIGHTFOLD PATH OF ADULT SELF-CARE

When we follow the practices on the eightfold path, we contribute to our own well-being and promote the health of everyone within our school community.

The practices on the eightfold path of adult self-care are:

1. Right View
2. Right Intention
3. Right Speech
4. Right Action
5. Right Livelihood
6. Right Effort
7. Right Mindfulness
8. Right Concentration

While some of the practices on the eightfold path are reminiscent of the seven grown-up skills (chapter 3), they differ principally in that they help us attend to our *own* needs, not just to the needs of our teenager students.

PRACTICE 1: RIGHT VIEW

The first thing we must do to take care of ourselves is see things as they are. We must adopt a *right view* of the situation, as Buddha taught. What does this mean in the teenage world?

Acknowledge the Power of Adolescence

First, we should acknowledge that the phenomenon of adolescence is real and that sometimes it has an infectious quality to it, and that no one is immune from getting swept up in the teenage fever. On the other hand, we should also feel confident that we can handle the adolescent dynamo when it hits and emerge better and stronger for it. Becoming affected in our relationships with teenagers is an important crucible in our work, and our work is a whole lot easier when we understand this point.

Cultivate Self-Awareness

Second, we should cultivate self-awareness and understand our vulnerabilities and challenges in our work with teenagers. It is not enough to understand the general principles of how adolescents behave. We must understand what happens to us personally when we get swept up in the adolescent drama. Some of us may consider case studies from previous chapters, and say to ourselves, "Well, that would never happen to me. I don't have to worry about that." And we may be right. But we all have to worry about *something*, and that's the point.

Adolescent Experiences: Middle and High School

A good place to start this practice of self-awareness is to reflect upon our own experiences during adolescence. We all survived the teenage world ourselves, and therefore we all have significant experience dealing with the challenges of adolescence. This personal history informs our present work with students and can provide us with clues about how we might be affected in our relationships with teenagers. The following questions are intended to help us develop self-awareness and think about our vulnerabilities in our relationship with teenagers:

1. What did you like about middle and high school? What did you dislike about your school experiences?
2. What kind of student were you? Where did you excel academically? In what areas were you challenged?
3. What kinds of recognition did you receive from your teachers or the school community? What role did you play within the community?

4. In general, what kind of relationships did you have with your teachers? Who were your favorite teachers, and why? Which teachers did you dislike, and why?

5. How well did your school community suit your learning style and needs?

6. If you had to do it all over again (assuming you had the power and ability to determine these things for yourself), what would you alter about your school experiences, and why? What would you want to remain the same, and why?

Recognizing Assumptions

These questions should help us recognize some of our assumptions about our students and our work. The truth is school has a profound impact on all adolescents—from the quality of the education to the interaction with teachers to the food in the cafeteria—school is a huge deal. When we return to school as teachers, we bring with us the imprint of our own adolescent experiences and this affects us in every aspect of our professional work.

The Case of Barb

Barb, an experienced language arts teacher, spent her teenage years being the "good girl." She always did her work, helped her classmates with their homework, and was often the teacher's pet. She learned what her teachers wanted from her and went out of her way to give it to them. What she didn't learn, at least not as well, was how to get her own needs met and derive satisfaction from achieving goals she set for herself.

Barb never felt confident about her own desires or feelings, which is why she always worked so hard to please others. She also resented anyone who appeared to have an easy time of it, so she had difficulty in her relationships at work. Barb resented some of her colleagues and even her students, especially the "popular" ones, as she labeled them, because they didn't seem to work as hard as she did.

Like many of us who haven't fully examined our own experiences, Barb couldn't separate her past from her present, which not only caused her to suffer, it also increased her susceptibility to getting caught off guard in the teenage world. As soon as Barb started to work with teenagers, she slipped right back into her old patterns—only, things had changed; Barb was no longer a student. She no longer could be a teacher's pet, for instance, and therefore she didn't know how to get what she needed from her surroundings.

This is how Barb brought her own adolescent experiences into her work, and this is why she was vulnerable in her relationships. As long as she remained unaware of how she was projecting her own internal experiences onto the external world, Barb created the same scenario for herself again and again, and her difficulties continued.

The Point of Vulnerability

We all bring our own psychological stuff to our work in the teenage world, and this stuff serves as our point of vulnerability. The point of vulnerability is different for everyone. For Barb, it was her desire to please others and ignore her own needs. When our points of vulnerability come into contact with the drama of the teenage world we can lose perspective, stop practicing grown-up skills and start behaving like grown-olders, which is what happened with Barb.

When we are aware of our vulnerabilities we can identify problems as they arise and recover quickly. Barb could have taken care of herself if she'd understood this, but her ignorance of how and why she got frustrated in her relationships kept her vulnerable and miserable in her work. One of the things Barb needed to understand was how her own experiences during adolescence, especially her experience with her peers, created challenges for her in her work.

Peer Relationships

Not only did all of us go to school during adolescence, we all had to contend with our peers, and the impact of these relationships may cause challenges in our dynamic with teenagers. Our answers to the following questions can help us determine how our own adolescent experiences influence how we think about our work in the teenage world:

1. What social group, if any, did you belong to during middle and high school, and how did your affiliation with this group serve or not serve you?
2. How important were cliques in your school? How were you personally included or excluded from various social groups?

3. Who were your closest friends? What did you expect from your friendships? Who were the people you did not get along with, and why?
4. What kind of intimate/romantic relationships did you have during adolescence?
5. In what social situations did you feel confident? In what situations did you feel unconfident? Why?
6. How were you influenced by your friends and peers? How did you influence them? In what kinds of situations were you a leader? In what kinds of situations were you a follower?

Relationship to Authority

Another area we should explore to cultivate a *right view* is our relationship to authority, both in terms of what we thought as teenagers and what we think currently. Consider the following questions from past and present perspectives to get an idea of how your attitudes about authority inform your work:

1. How do teachers and administrators get along with each other in your school community? Under what circumstances does an us vs. them mentality arise within the adult environment?
2. How well do teenagers and adults get along?
3. How much trust and respect does each group afford one another?
4. In what circumstances do you feel empowered within your community? In what circumstances do you feel disempowered? Why?
5. How much autonomy do you have in your work? How satisfied are you with the autonomy you have? Would you like more, less?
6. How are decisions made within your community? How active a role do you play in decision making? How satisfied are you with the decision making process that exists?
7. In general, what do you think of authority? How well do you get along with your supervisors?

Recognizing Projections

The reason it is important to think about these questions, which on the surface may seem unrelated to our work, is that all of us understand our present situations based on our past experiences. It follows, then, that we bring to our current work various prejudices, beliefs, and ideas about what adolescence is like, or what it *should* be like, based on these personal experiences. This is projection.

Teachers need to think about projection because when we work in schools our past experiences get triggered all the time by our present environment. All adults project their past onto their present but most adults don't work in places that serve as constant reminders of their own past. It is only those who work in schools who work in the same place where they spent their formative years, so we need to think about how we project our formative experiences onto our work.

When we return to schools as professionals, we must be careful not to slip into the patterns we established during our own adolescence. Again, this may seem self-evident but attorneys, doctors—all other professionals, for that matter—don't work in surroundings that evoke their own adolescent experiences and memories on a daily basis. Those of us who work with teenagers do, and therefore we have to unlearn as much as we learn about our working environment in order to practice grown-up skills and be successful.

The Case of Jefferson

This was a critical issue for Jefferson, a middle-aged teacher who was oppositional by nature and described himself as a perpetual adolescent. Jefferson didn't have any interest in exploring his adolescent experiences because he was reliving them at work. For Jefferson, this meant bucking authority at every opportunity, which is developmentally appropriate for teenagers to do, but not adults. Jefferson took pride in his ability to ruffle the feathers of the powers that be, and he made sure never to ally with the administration if he could help it. When he did have to toe the line, Jefferson made certain his students knew that he was still on their side, and that he was still a rebel.

Jefferson liked working in schools because he was still living in the teenage world, at least in his own mind. Jefferson hadn't done the psychological work necessary to separate his past from his present, and because he was surrounded by teenagers every day he thought he could get away with it, or rather, he didn't think about it at all. Jefferson was completely unapologetic about his behavior and, more to the point, completely unreflective.

Jefferson didn't realize that he was a patsy, though, because he was so committed to remaining a teenager himself. Jefferson's students knew he would always do their bidding, which is how he got manipulated by them; this was his personal point of vulnerability. For example, when his students were upset with the administration for enforcing rules or consequences, Jefferson lead the rallying cry. Jefferson was the de facto student representative on the faculty, which would have been appropriate if he had actually represented their interests. But he didn't, of course, because he couldn't. Jefferson never really represented his students' best interests because he only knew how to represent his own, therefore his students were patsies too.

Jefferson shared a vulnerability with many adults who work in the teenage world, which is he really liked the teenage world, so much so that he never wanted to leave it. Jefferson wasn't satisfied being immersed in this world throughout the day; he wanted to be in it always. Most of us who work in schools do so, in part, because we liked being in school ourselves. It's rare to find a teacher who truly hated being in school. So those of us who choose to work in schools may be motivated by a desire to return to our pleasant past experiences. This was Jefferson's motivation, although he didn't know it, and that was his challenge. When this is one of our motives for working in the teenage world we must acknowledge it, and we must recognize that working in school is different than being in school, a distinction Jefferson needed to make.

Jefferson also needed the assistance of someone who could help him make this distinction, and who could encourage him to enjoy his work but at the same time differentiate himself from his teenage students. Because Jefferson had been teaching for years, it would take him time and support to understand a suitable role for himself in the teenage world, and thus to care for himself appropriately. Jefferson needed to be convinced that membership in the grown-up world has its advantages, and that practicing grown-up skills would allow him to manage the teenage world more effectively than while we was still identified with it.

Career Expectations and Satisfaction

Jefferson didn't know how to care for himself, and he also didn't know how to gauge his expectations for his career, which is part of self-care. Jefferson got a lot of satisfaction from his job, though, but for reasons that left him and his students vulnerable. Had he examined himself and considered what he expected and wanted, Jefferson might have discovered that teaching wasn't the profession for him. Or he might have discovered the opposite: He might have realized that he could practice grown-up skills and enjoy teaching at the same time. Either way, by practicing *right view*, Jefferson could have determined if he was headed in the right direction, which is essential for self-care.

Because career expectations and satisfaction are important aspects of *right view*, we owe it to ourselves to determine whether we are in the right place, professionally speaking. To this end, I suggest we take stock of our professional situation every few years and ask ourselves the following questions to determine if our experiences at work match the expectations we have for our career:

1. How much satisfaction do you get from your work? Are there other things you want to do professionally? If so, what plans are you making to satisfy these ambitions?
2. Do you routinely establish and achieve professional goals? What expectations do you have for your work and how do these translate into concrete and definite plans for your professional future? Who in your work community has a stake in your professional success and supports your professional goals?
3. If you had to do your career path over again, what would you do differently? If there are things you would do differently, how does this inform the professional path you are now on?
4. What did you expect when you first starting working in the teenage world? Which expectations have been met? Which haven't?
5. How well does your current school community support your professional goals? Is this community a good fit for you? If not, what steps do you take to support yourself within the community, and have you considered joining another school community that is more personally and professionally compatible?
6. Is being an adult in the teenage world the right profession for you? Why or why not?

The Professional Satisfaction Pie

When I speak to new teachers, I use a pie chart to help them think about their professional goals and satisfaction. I explain that we need to satisfy about seven out of ten pieces of the *professional satisfaction pie* in order to continue to feel good about what we're doing. We must determine which seven slices are important to us—everyone's satisfaction chart is different—and which are essential for our career satisfaction. This process of discrimination inevitably implies compromise—we can't always get what we want—but we must get enough of what we want or we risk feeling embittered and dissatisfied in our work.

I recommend adults create such a chart and refer to it annually as part of a professional and personal review. Such a review is part of the practice of *right view* and helps us determine what we need to maintain our self-care. The following is a list of possible slices for the professional satisfaction pie:

1. Salary, Benefits
2. Work Schedule, Work Load
3. School Philosophy/Mission—Personal Compatibility with Community Values
4. Collegial Relationships, Relationship with Administration
5. Relationship with Students and Parents
6. Potential for Professional Growth, Professional Development Opportunities
7. Social Status
8. Professional Status
9. Degree of Professional Collaboration/Autonomy
10. Compatibility of Career with Personal Goals and Aspirations

Everyone will have different ingredients in their pie, but all of us must get a certain degree of satisfaction from our work in order to do our jobs well. If we can determine what we must have in order to feel satisfied, then we can chart and measure our progress, which is part of the practice of self-care.

No Job Is Perfect

No job is perfect and no job can meet all our needs, but the right job should meet enough of them to keep us going. When we adopt a *right view* of our professional situation, using something like the professional satisfaction pie to keep track of our needs, we should maintain a sense

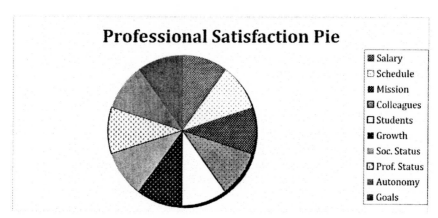

Professional Satisfaction Pie

- Salary
- Schedule
- Mission
- Colleagues
- Students
- Growth
- Soc. Status
- Prof. Status
- Autonomy
- Goals

Figure 7.1.

of joy and satisfaction in our work. On the other hand, we must also be realistic about what we expect from any job, and prioritize those things that are most important to ensure good self-care.

Burnout

In my experience, teachers don't talk much about burnout. I'm not sure why. Maybe it's because we think teaching is such an honorable profession and therefore to talk about burnout dishonors our work. Or maybe we think our students couldn't live without us, so taking time off or leaving the profession isn't an option. Or maybe we fear disappointing our colleagues, or even ourselves, if we admit to feeling burned out. Whatever the reason, I think adults who work in schools should be encouraged to talk about burnout without fear of recrimination from the community. Recognizing when we feel depleted by our work is part of the practice of *right view*, so we shouldn't neglect this important topic.

There are four warning signs of burnout that adults should keep in mind, and when we experience any of them, we should consider whether burnout is the cause:

1. Loss of energy or enthusiasm for work, feelings of depression surrounding work. When we feel these things for extended periods of time, and when these feelings don't correspond to specific or obvious stressors, then burnout may be a factor.

2. Negativity. If we aren't naturally negative people, or even if we are, and we find ourselves being overridingly negative about work, burnout might be the cause. Sometimes teenagers can be very negative and we can pick this up, but we should be able to recover when we're removed from the situation, or when we get a break from work. But when nothing about work seems positive to us, something is wrong.

3. Not invested in relationships. Ideally, we should feel invigorated and challenged by our relationships at work. Teaching is one of the most relational professions around, so when we start divesting from our relationships, or when we feel too depleted to give anything of ourselves in our relationships, we should pay attention.

4. Excess stress or worry about work. Another sign of burnout is unremitting stress or anxiety. When we don't recover from routine work stressors, like grading exams or other consuming duties, burnout might be the cause.

When we experience any of the above symptoms it's time to pay attention and practice self-care. When routine self-care doesn't improve our situation, and when we can't identify other causes for our symptoms, then it's time to consider whether we are burned out. In such cases, we should find someone to talk to about our circumstances, and hopefully we can share our concerns with someone at work. When schools and administrators think proactively about burnout problems get identified early, and measures can be taken to support teachers in getting help. When this happens, teachers are less likely to leave the profession or, if they do, chances are greater they will return in a few years feeling refreshed and enthusiastic.

When we engage in all of the above practices, like examining how our past influences our present; recognizing our vulnerabilities in our work; understanding what it is we really want from work, we practice *right view*, and this is good self-care.

PRACTICE 2: RIGHT INTENTION

The second practice of the eightfold path is *right intention*, which is sometimes interpreted by Buddhists as *right thought*. For our purposes, *right intention* is the practice of attending to our thoughts and moods throughout the day. This practice helps us to be purposeful and not reactive in our thinking. When we are intentional about our mental states, we determine our experiences to a great degree, which is an important element of self-care.

Teenagers Are All Over the Map

Why is it important to be intentional about our mental states? Because teenage thoughts and emotions are all over the map, and they spread like wildfire. When we catch the mood of teenagers we can get entangled in their world. To take care of ourselves, then, we should understand not only how to track our own thoughts and moods but also how to separate our internal processes from those of our students.

The Case of Marissa

Marissa's story is a prime example of how we can lose our bearings in the midst of teenage emotion. One day after class, Marissa, a fine arts teacher, was approached by a posse of 8th grade girls. One of the girls was clearly upset—her face was red and she had been crying—and the other five girls were there to lend support.

When Marissa asked them what was wrong, all six answered in unison, creating a conversational maelstrom. Each girl tried to out-shout the others in an attempt to get Marissa's attention, and therefore it took a while for Marissa to understand what was going on. But it didn't take long for her to *feel* what was going on—Marissa caught on to that instantly.

The girls were upset, Marissa discovered, because one of their friends, who they didn't want to name initially, had developed an eating disorder, or so they believed. The girls reported to Marissa that their friend ate only lettuce at lunch and was getting too thin. As the girls continued, they became increasingly upset and agitated, and a few more of them began to cry. Finally, one of them blurted out, "I'm sooooo worried about her! My mom is a psychiatrist and she thinks so-and-so has a huge problem and that her parents are in denial. I think so too because I know her parents and they can't deal with anything."

As Marissa listened to the story, she became more and more agitated herself. She knew how pernicious eating disorders can be, and she also knew that there were already a number of girls in the 8th grade who had been identified as having eating disorders. She felt the rising panic of the group of girls and began to feel helpless, as if she were in their emotional grasp. Marissa also felt uncertain about how to calm the girls down, and was therefore relieved when Claire, a fellow teacher, entered the room.

Claire joined the conversation at Marissa's request and instantly felt the tsunami of hysteria-ladened information flood around her. Claire, too, became increasingly upset in response, especially because she taught the student in question (whose name had been inadvertently blurted out) and hadn't seen any of this coming. She asked the girls a series of questions about their suspicions and soon became convinced that her student was in dire circumstances. She even started to tear up a bit as the girls spoke about their friend.

Now both Marissa and Claire felt helpless and panicked, and neither knew what to do. Because they had been so affected by their students' emotions and thought processes, it was as if they had lost track of their own—and they had, to a degree. Amid the drama created by the group, Marissa and Claire summarily agreed with the girls' assessment of the situation and also agreed, at the girls' urging, to speak with their friend about her problem. With the high pitch of teenage emotion ringing in their ears, Marissa and Claire overrode their own cognitive processes and summoned the identified student, whom they now feared was teetering on the precipice of life.

Without pausing to reflect on what was happening, Marissa and Claire approached the student in question and shared their concerns. They described to her the conversation they had had with her friends, assured her they would help (without any plan in mind), and looked for her reaction. Not surprisingly, instead of diffusing the situation, they merely amped it up, and in the process they had unwittingly served as vectors for the adolescent virus. Now they had seven hysterical students on their hands, and no solution to the problem in sight.

Suffice to say, Marissa and Claire did not practice *right intention* during their conversations with their students. While they experienced various emotions and thoughts during the discussions, their reactions weren't entirely their own. This is not to suggest that their experiences were wrong, or that they should have been unaffected by what was being reported. No, their feelings were genuine, but they were inflamed—they had been trampled by the powerful force of the adolescent herd.

In order to take care of themselves, and thus to take care of their students and the problem at hand, Marissa and Claire needed to remain clear about their own mental processes and how these differed from their students' experience. If what teenagers need from adults is their ability to respond and to not react, then what we need from ourselves is the ability to practice *right intention*.

By keeping track of our own thoughts and feelings, and by weighing them against our students' perspectives, we see through the chaos of the moment and bring order to the teenage situation. Had Marissa and Claire practiced *right intention*, they would have recognized that their own thoughts and feelings got lost in the fever pitch of their students' reactions, and until they got in touch with their own adult responses they couldn't intervene effectively.

For what it's worth, Marissa and Claire were both very competent and thoughtful teachers, and neither was prone to overreaction. They were, however, susceptible to the power of teenage feelings, as we all are, and neither had thought much about how to take care of themselves when faced with such an onslaught of emotion. This increased the probability that they might dismiss their own adult reactions when faced with a surge of teenage near-hysteria, which is exactly what happened. Because they took their students' reactions to the situation at face value and didn't check in with themselves—or with each other—about what was going on in their own minds, they not only got themselves into an emotional tizzy, but they spread that tizzy around.

At the end of the day, not only did Marissa and Claire have a mess to clean up, they were also emotionally strung out and exhausted. What could they have done differently in this situation? How could they have taken better care of themselves and their students in the moment? And what would have constituted *right intention*?

Questions to Stay on Track

I encourage adults to consider the following questions when faced with charged situations in the teenage world. These questions should help us stay in touch with our own thoughts and feelings and proceed

based on our own perspective, not on what we're picking up from a
febrile teenage world:

1. Is this an emergency situation? If so, what needs to be done to
   contain the situation, and what other adults in the community
   should be informed and/or can help?
       This question invites its corollary, which is, what constitutes
   an emergency? Does the situation involve loss of blood and/or
   consciousness? If so, then the situation is probably serious. If not,
   adults probably have some time to respond.[1]
2. If this is not an emergency, what can be done to deescalate the
   emotional reactions of the parties involved? Is the situation com-
   pounded by multiple reactions? Would the situation be contained
   more effectively if individuals were dealt with separately rather
   than as a group?
3. What additional information must be gathered to comprehensively
   assess the situation? How should the assessment proceed, and who
   should carry out the assessment?
4. How well do adult and teenage reactions match in this situation?
   (If they are identical or closely allied, chances are good the adults
   involved may have lost some of their perspective.) How would the
   adult emotional response and plan of action differ if this scenario
   was stripped of its teenage emotional and cognitive content? In
   other words, how might the adult reaction change if just the "facts"
   were presented?
5. How effectively do adult responses serve to manage the situation?
   What is the nature of the aftermath? Is there evidence of an adult
   emotional "hangover"?
6. What could be done differently in this situation, and how could
   adult reactions, when practiced with *right intention*, inform the
   assessment and plan of action?

Know Thyself

When we practice *right intention*, we consider these questions and
manage to check in with our own thoughts and feelings as situations in
the teenage world unfold. When we get caught up in the wildfire like
Marissa and Claire did, *right intention* allows us to turn down the flame

and bring a measure of rationality and calm to the fore. It enables us to take care of ourselves because we check in with ourselves, differentiate our experiences from those of our students, and get out of the teenage fire as quickly as possible. This reduces our exposure to the feverish aspects of adolescence and keeps us healthy in the long run.

PRACTICE 3: RIGHT SPEECH

The practice of *right speech* means pretty much what it says. This practice addresses how we speak in the teenage world, a place where speech can be vicious, and encourages us to be mindful of what we say and how we say it. Teenagers have a tendency to hear everything, especially when it's spoken by adults, and we shouldn't lose sight of this fact. (This is not to suggest that teenagers *listen* to everything that's said, or that they *heed* what is said—that's another story. But they definitely *hear* what is said.) The practice of *right speech* helps us stay clear about our role with teenagers, and this helps us maintain the boundaries between us and them that ensure our well-being.

Talking about Students

Here's an unavoidable truth about the teenage world: Many, if not all of us, talk about our students on occasion, and I don't mean we discuss how well our students are doing in class. This is a natural tendency—one we should acknowledge. All adults talk about work, and because we work with students, sometimes we talk about them. But beware: This can be very risky business, as Benecio learned the hard way.

The Case of Benecio

Benecio, a young science teacher, was chaperoning a field trip when he found himself engaged in a conversation with a colleague. His colleague asked Benecio his opinion of some students in his class and without thinking Benecio gave an uncensored answer. What Benecio didn't realize, much to his regret and embarrassment, was that he and his colleague were in ear shot of a student, who promptly reported the details of the conversation to her classmates. Had Benecio remembered to practice *right speech*, he could have avoided a huge mess, which he spent weeks mopping up.

Benecio did not intend to gossip about his students, and he didn't, really. He just said the wrong thing at the wrong time. But sometimes our speech about students does get gossipy, and this can be very hazardous for everyone within the community.

The Case of Rafael

Rafael was a popular coach and teacher who often bantered playfully with his male athletes on the soccer field. At times, this banter was of the locker room variety, and sometimes it involved students who weren't present, specifically female students. Rafael never initiated these conversations but neither did he guide his athletes away from such topics. Rafael was known among students as someone who had a high tolerance for inappropriate language, which is why they felt comfortable including him in their conversations, both on and off the field.

One day, Joe, a senior on the soccer team, emailed Rafael an inappropriate comment about a female classmate. Without thinking, Rafael answered the email in the lax manner he used on the field. While Joe thought Rafael's response was hilarious, Joe's father didn't. Joe inadvertently left his email open and within hours the evidence of Rafael's wrong speech was in the principal's office.

Rafael's transgression got him into a lot of trouble, but the truth is, despite his poor judgment, Rafael wasn't a spiteful guy. He was just careless about his speech and he got caught. Any of us could have made the same mistake Rafael made, in one form or another, which is why we all should examine how we talk about students.

Student-Free Zones

Of course, sometimes it is important for us to talk about students. Before these conversations take place, however, we should ensure that we are in student-free zones, where students or other adults cannot overhear conversations. In addition, I suggest we ask ourselves before these conversations take place, What's the purpose of the discussion? Who does it serve, us or our student? If the conversation doesn't serve students, chances are good it won't serve us in the long run, either. If we must engage in non-work-related conversations about students, I suggest we do it after hours, off school grounds, and in a private place. In addition, we should never assume, even under these circumstances, that the contents of the conversation will remain private.

When we practice *right speech* we care for ourselves and create safe environments for our students, and we stay out of trouble.

PRACTICE 4: RIGHT ACTION

Right action is the practice of behaviors that keep us physically and emotionally healthy. *Right action* covers our basic needs, those things we shouldn't live without but often do because of the demands of our work in the teenage world.

Basic Physical Needs: Good Food, Sleep, Exercise

All of us who work in the teenage world should take care of our basic physical needs like sleeping, exercising, and eating well. This sounds simple but many of us don't do it for a variety of reasons. We must attend to our basic needs if we want to create communities that are productive and conducive to learning, but this takes time, a precious commodity in schools. Many of us wager we can catch up on lost sleep and exercise on the weekend and during the summer, but this is a costly gamble. We must keep pace with teenage energy levels, and this requires a prudent and quotidian routine of self-care. If nothing else, we should give ourselves permission to prioritize our basic needs. If we don't, nobody else will. We should also be prepared to defend our right to take care of ourselves.

The Case of Beth

Beth, an experienced debate coach, had to do just that, but it wasn't comfortable or easy at times. Beth took a brisk walk around the school's athletic fields every day in an effort to get a little exercise and to clear her mind. Beth was vigilant about meeting her work commitments but she also was committed to taking a much-needed break during the school day. She was an exemplary employee and chalked up much of her success to her practice of *right action*.

Beth's behavior came under the scrutiny of her colleagues because it was out in the open and, as a result, she was often forced to defend herself, or rather, she was forced to suffer the comments that can abound in tight communities. Why did *she* get to take a break when her colleagues were slaving away? Why were *her* needs so important that she was allowed to attend to them every day?

Because Beth worked in a community where many adults had trouble advocating for themselves and their legitimate needs, her behavior was sometimes misunderstood as selfish. But it wasn't selfish, it was her practice of *right action*, and it was something many of her colleagues needed to practice for themselves. In order for them to feel such behavior was acceptable, Beth and her colleagues needed the leadership of administrators who understood the importance of *right action* and proactive self-care.

Basic Emotional Needs: Love, Connection, Community

Those of us who work in schools are sometimes prone to sacrificing our emotional needs for our work, or of trying to get our emotional needs met at work rather than outside of work. This is especially true at boarding schools, although it needn't be, but it is an occupational hazard in day schools as well. When our work community is our only community, we're not practicing *right action*.

Schools are places where feelings of connection, community, and affection are natural, particularly among students, and where everyone is encouraged to cheer for the home team, so to speak. As a result, many of us develop powerful feelings of attachment to our students, colleagues, and institutions. This is normal, even desired, really, because it means we are connected and committed to our work. But it's not sufficient, at least not in terms of meeting our basic emotional needs. We also need to experience love, connection, and community beyond the confines of work, otherwise we risk looking to work to satisfy things it can't and simply shouldn't satisfy. As teachers, we invariably receive lots of attention and affection from our students, but we mustn't forget to get these needs met elsewhere too. Kellon didn't do this and he paid a big price for it.

The Case of Kellon

Kellon worked in schools his whole career. He loved schools and he loved the people in them. Kellon was satisfied spending his free time going to athletic events, attending student plays and concerts, and chaperoning student clubs. Some of this was expected, if not required of him, and all of it was appreciated by his principal, who was happy to have someone as well liked and capable as Kellon in attendance. Furthermore, it made Kellon and his students happy. Wasn't that enough?

Not in the summer it wasn't, when Kellon was prone to depression and forced to feel the void in his life, a void created and simultaneously filled by his dedication to his work. As Kellon approached retirement, his stress increased. He had spent years investing in a relationship with a community that couldn't pay dividends in the long run, and he didn't realize it until it was too late. When we don't get our needs for love and intimacy met, chances are good we'll feel depressed and stressed out, much like Kellon did.

Stress: The New Cultural Currency

Kellon was stressed, but not in a way we usually think about stress in schools. Nevertheless, his stress was real and he couldn't deal with it. Stress has become one of the most important cultural currencies in many schools. At high-performing schools and among high-performing teenagers, stress is expected, even bragged about. This is true among adult populations too, and it's becoming a serious problem. While emotions such as anger and depression are rarely acknowledged, stress is often considered *de rigueur*. In some communities, when adults and students *aren't* stressed out, something fishy is going on. Think about it: When was the last time you heard a colleague talk about feeling relaxed at work?

Stress is not a categorically bad thing, of course, but excessive or unremitting stress is. Our bodies can handle lots of stress—bodies are designed to manage stress, and we need stress to perform well—but our bodies also need to relax regularly and to recover from bouts of stressful activity. Without periods of regular relaxation, the body and mind grow weary, and performance drops. Beth knew this instinctively: She used her daily walks to relax her mind and to burn off the stressful energy that had accumulated in her body throughout the school day. Unfortunately, many adults don't manage their stress as effectively as Beth did and, as a result, they return home at the end of the day feeling exhausted.

Managing stress is a fairly straightforward proposition from a physiological standpoint, but acknowledging that it should be done and working it into the workday routine is another matter. We find all kinds of excuses to not take care of ourselves in this way, even passing up opportunities when they present themselves during the work day.

The Case of Josh

Josh was a third-year teacher who felt overwhelmed by his duties and was unable to seize the moment when it came to relaxing on occasion during the school day. Josh feared if he let his guard down for even a moment, he wouldn't complete all his tasks, and he worried that his performance wasn't good enough as it was. Josh also felt he needed to impress his colleagues, even if that meant working himself ragged. Josh refused to relax regardless of the circumstance, even when those around him were doing so.

Not surprisingly, Josh was not a happy camper: He felt irritated much of the time and was unable to replenish his energy or enthusiasm, even after a vacation break. Because he couldn't manage his stress, Josh put his effectiveness and his future as a teacher at risk. But how was Josh supposed to squeeze in relaxation time at work? Good question, one that many schools are seriously addressing now that stress is pervading the culture.

Relaxation Tips

In order to relieve stress and to relax, the body needs to activate its *relaxation response*.[2] The relaxation response is the physiological antithesis of the fight-or-flight or stress response, and the two systems cannot be engaged at the same time. Once the relaxation response kicks in, stress is relieved, so it's important to know how to activate this physiological stress-buster. Learning how to relax is a crucial part of *right action*, and all of us should create routines for stress reduction we can use throughout the school day.

Many schools are now taking the issue of stress and relaxation very seriously, and some teachers are introducing relaxation exercises into their daily practice with students. Schools are also looking to organizations like the Benson-Henry Institute (B-HI) of Mind Body Medicine for guidance in developing school-wide stress-reduction initiatives. These initiatives introduce all members of the community to relaxation techniques, but the B-HI in particular believes that adults must adopt these practices first, before we can use them effectively with our students. Researchers at the B-HI understand that we can't teach what we haven't mastered, so when they work with schools they focus on the adults first, not the students. This is an example of *right action* in practice. (See the appendix for stress reduction and relaxation exercises.)

PRACTICE 5: RIGHT LIVELIHOOD

The practice of *right livelihood* is a given for adults who work in the teenage world. Teaching is a noble profession and we should feel proud of what we do. Taking pride in our work and feeling invested are important for self-care and allow us to weather the ups and downs of the teenage world. I think most of us do feel proud of what we do, but not everyone in this culture values teaching the way they should, which became clear to me one day on my way to work.

I was running late one morning, so I hopped into a cab and blurted out the directions to my school. The cab driver, a recent immigrant from Vietnam, asked, "Are you a teacher?" And while technically I wasn't—I was a school counselor at the time—I said yes in an effort to simplify the conversation and because I *had* been a teacher at various points along the way. Apparently I gave the right answer, though, because my driver spent the next ten minutes in a veritable reverie about teachers. I had never heard anyone speak of teachers in such hallowed terms before. It was amazing and it made me feel great.

What was most amazing, however, was that I realized that for all the rhetoric in mainstream American culture about the importance of teachers, I had never heard anything like this before. My cab driver was in awe of teachers, and he meant every word of it. He gushed when he talked about how important teachers were in his country, and in what high esteem they are held. He got so into it that he almost didn't let me pay for my cab ride.

I often wonder why Americans don't value teachers the way my cab driver did, and what teachers can do about it. Teachers don't rank in cultures where money is an important indicator of success, and as a result those of us who teach may not believe our work is valued. Teachers are among the lowest paid white-collar professionals, and the ceiling on potential earnings is relatively low, even for the best and the brightest. Our culture doesn't put its money where its mouth is when it comes to education, and that sends us a very powerful message about its perceived worth.

In cultures where wisdom is valued over money—or where wisdom is valued *period*, even apart from money—teachers are held in very high regard, and this goes a long way to compensate for the salary gap, in my opinion. I can testify after my short cab ride how great it feels to be seen as professionally relevant, and this feeling contributes to self-care.

Find a Mentor

Because our culture doesn't give teachers the recognition we deserve, we must find it for ourselves. To this end, I suggest we find mentors within the profession, colleagues we admire and to whom we can turn for support. The purpose of a mentor, apart from providing practical help, is to serve as a role model, and perhaps even as a hero when necessary. Everyone needs someone to look up to, especially those of us who serve as role models all day long. I believe when we admire someone in our profession we are more likely to value our own work, and this is an important aspect of the practice of *right livelihood*.

Administrators can help this effort by establishing mentoring programs in their schools. Ideally, these programs should have a broad focus, and should extend beyond mentoring only new teachers. Mid and late career teachers need support and mentoring too, albeit of a different nature. Not only do such programs support the adults who receive mentoring, they also provide opportunities for master teachers to help their colleagues, and to create roles for themselves that extend beyond the classroom. Sometimes it's not enough to be valued by teenagers. A good mentoring program allows veteran teachers, and those with specific talents, to be valued within their communities in a different way. A good mentoring program is like a wisdom bank, with community members making deposits or withdrawals depending on their circumstances and need.

PRACTICE 6: RIGHT EFFORT

The practice of *right effort* is critical to those of us who teach, a profession that breeds workaholism on one end of the performance scale and complacency on the other. Knowing how to strike a balance between the two extremes is perhaps the most fundamental and yet profound skill for us to practice in our quest for self-care, and this is what *right effort* is all about.

Workaholism

One of the worst occupational hazards of teaching is workaholism, which often results in us feeling bitter, burned out, and ineffective. Unfortunately many school communities reward workaholism, and high-performing schools fairly breed it among students and adults alike. In fact, workaholism has become so common in certain schools, especially in schools with high performing parents, that it's considered the gold standard of achievement. Any effort that falls short of the workaholic threshold is considered unacceptable in these communities, and this makes workaholism very hard to combat.

One sure sign we are out of balance when it comes to *right effort* is when we get preoccupied with work. We must have regular down time in order to be effective and to take care of ourselves, and those of us who work all the time pay the price eventually. Unfortunately, workaholism tends to persist; it doesn't just go away by itself.

I once heard the following exchange take place between a veteran teacher and a newcomer at a faculty retreat. It was clear that the newcomer, who felt overwhelmed in his job, was looking for guidance about how to balance his life and hoped that he wouldn't feel overwhelmed forever. In effect, he was looking for advice on *right effort*. The exchange went like this:

New teacher: What do you do in your free time?

Veteran teacher: Work.

New teacher: What do you do for fun?

Veteran teacher: Work.

New teacher: What do you do on the weekend?

Veteran teacher: Work.

Needless to say, the new teacher didn't get any helpful insights on how to balance his life, although he learned a lot about his new school culture because his colleague was one of the most respected and revered members of the faculty.

Beware Martyrdom

Workaholics risk becoming martyrs if they're not careful, although not all martyrs are workaholics, by any means. *Martyr* in this case refers to someone who suffers in the extreme; while all teachers suffer at some point in their work, there's suffering and then there's *suffering*, a self-inflicted wound that is the defining feature of the martyr.

The Case of Dolores

Dolores was a classic workaholic martyr. She gave everything to her work, and during her two decades teaching she sacrificed all she had for her job and her students. She taught more classes than was required by her department, served on every possible committee, volunteered for every thankless job available, and even agreed to proctor afterschool events when she didn't have to. Dolores did it all. Then she felt miserable.

When anyone suggested to Dolores that she did too much, she gave a weak smile and said she was happy with her lot. She said she wanted to work this hard. She said the school needed her to do what she did. Dolores convinced herself that if she didn't pick up the slack, the school would collapse. So, she kept on working herself to the bone and complaining about it.

Dolores confused *right effort* with endless effort, which are very different things. She didn't know the first thing about *right effort*, and because she was a martyr she didn't care. Dolores's purpose in life was to suffer and complain, and by this measure she was a success. But she took awful care of herself and in the process she alienated her colleagues and students.

Dolores was not alone in wanting to give her best effort at work. Most of us do. Most of us avoid Dolores's fate, however, because we simply tire out. Those of us who do succumb to excessive effort should get help to manage our duties. True, Dolores was a martyr, but she wasn't born a martyr, which means chances were good she could unlearn her behavior, provided she got some encouragement from a supervisor. Sometimes those of us who are like Dolores need someone in authority to intervene and tell us that we can't do something, not simply that we shouldn't.

The Case of Raymond

Raymond's problem was that he couldn't summon up the effort to do anything; he was the professional opposite of Dolores. Raymond had years of experience under his belt and his performance was adequate, but he stayed in cruise control most of the time. He didn't invest in improving his curriculum or lesson plans because he didn't see the point. Although he was interested in his subject matter, he wasn't interested enough to learn more about it, plus he worked at a school with lots of chaos, so it was easy for him to neglect his work and get away with it.

Raymond's lack of *right effort* was a disservice to himself and his students, and it demonstrated that he didn't practice self-care very well. *Right effort* is as much about pushing oneself as it is about not pushing oneself over the edge—although Raymond didn't want to push himself at all. As a result, he took little pride in what he did and never felt a sense of accomplishment. Apart from the fact that pride and accomplishment are things we try to instill in our students—and so we should model it—Raymond let himself down. He was a smart, educated professional who just didn't care anymore. Something was wrong, and his lack of *right effort* was the indicator.

Chances are good Raymond's lack of care was masking something more serious, maybe burnout or even depression. When we feel like Raymond did, it's an indication that we need much more self-care, and perhaps the help of a mentor. When administrators notice a decline in teacher effort, they should support teachers to identify a cause and get the help they need.

Teenagers experience enough martyrdom and complacency in their own lives; the last thing they need is to be surrounded by adults who feel the same way. Instead, *right effort* is what teenagers need to see, and *right effort* is what we need to practice in order to take care of ourselves. It takes time to master, though, and success is hard to gauge. That said, when we practice *right effort* we should feel invigorated by work and refreshed by leisure, and we should feel satisfied a lot of the time.

PRACTICES 7 AND 8: RIGHT MINDFULNESS
AND RIGHT CONCENTRATION

The final practices for adult self-care in the teenage world are *right mindfulness* and *right concentration*, which when combined mean positive thinking. When we think positively about our work, we promote our well-being and resilience. Trite as it may sound, positivity pays great dividends in the teenage world, where adolescent negativity and cynicism run rampant.

The Power of Positive Thinking

When we practice self-care we tend to feel positive, and when we feel positive when tend to care for ourselves better. When we are positive in our outlook and speech, we create environments that foster positivity in others. While it might be too optimistic to think our positivity can make our students positive, a positive attitude helps. When I suggest a positive attitude as part of self-care for adults, I don't mean to suggest that we should ignore our problems or pretend to feel something that we don't. Instead, I believe we have a right to feel good a lot of the time, so if we don't we should commit ourselves to figuring out what's wrong. The clarion call to positivity is not about putting a good face on things, although this helps at times. It's about claiming our right to feel good and taking ourselves and our problems seriously when we don't.

When we practice good self-care in the teenage world, we tend to like ourselves and our teenage students, feel good about what we do and how we live, and enjoy our work. The practices of *right mindfulness* and *right concentration* remind us that we have a right, even a responsibility, to feel good about what we do. When we don't feel good, something's wrong. So positivity, then, is as much a gauge of how well we're taking care of ourselves as it is a state of mind. If we don't feel generally happy about our work, it's time to raise the ante of self-care.

THE ADMINISTRATOR'S ROLE
ON THE EIGHTFOLD PATH

Most of us who work in the teenage world are smart, competent, and hardworking, but that doesn't mean we don't need help to reach our potential, and to take care of ourselves along the way. The administrator's role in the eightfold path is that of companion and guide. Administrators are our companions because they share our burdens in the teenage world, and they are also our guides because it is their job to lead us in our quest to be healthy and effective professionals. I encourage administrators to think about how they can support adults to this end, and to consider ways to establish and promote self-care initiatives for all faculty and staff, using the eightfold path as a reference point.

EXERCISES AND REFLECTIONS

1. How would you rate your ability to take care of yourself, in and outside of work?
2. What specific practices of self-care do you engage in regularly?
3. What happened the last time you neglected to take care of yourself? How did you deal with the situation and how did you get yourself back into balance?
4. How would you rate your community's attitude toward self-care? What does your school do to promote adult self-care? What messages do you receive about self-care and do any of them contradict one another?
5. How do you model self-care to students, and how and when do you talk to them about self-care?
6. How satisfied are you with your work and your school community? How would you rate your relationships with colleagues? What would you change about these things if you could?
7. What advice would you give to a newcomer to your community about taking care of themselves, and what does your advice say about your school culture?

CHAPTER SUMMARY

Those of us who work in the teenage world must take care of ourselves in order to do our jobs effectively. The eightfold path to self-care is a set of practices that promote self-awareness and self-care for adults, and ideally each practice brings us increased satisfaction in our work with teenagers.

NOTES

1. I use the threshold of blood and loss of consciousness to determine emergencies but obviously emergencies come in all forms, and therefore my criteria shouldn't be taken literally. I use these criteria as a shorthand way to gauge the seriousness of a situation in the teenage world, where not-so-serious situations tend to gain momentum quickly. What can feel like an emergency to a teenager is often not an emergency from an adult perspective, and adult judgment must prevail in order to bring balance to an out-of-balance situation.

2. Dr. Herbert Benson, a pioneer in mind-body medicine and the study of stress, coined the term *relaxation response*. Benson is the founder of the Benson-Henry Institute for Mind Body Medicine (Massachusetts General Hospital, Boston, www.mbmi. org) and the author of *The Relaxation Response*. He is an associate professor at Harvard Medical School and has done extensive work to bring relaxation techniques to students and teachers in schools.

Epilogue

THE CASE OF NATALIE

Natalie's 12th grade English class was filled with bright and eager students. Sam wasn't one of them. Sam was a surly, often oppositional student, and he didn't perform well most of the time. Natalie could see that Sam had some talent—occasionally he handed in a very good essay—but it was clear that he wasn't interested in doing well in her class.

Natalie met with all of her students in one-on-one conferences at least once a month. She really enjoyed this part of her work because it gave her the chance to get to know her students better and give them individual help. Natalie dreaded her conferences with Sam, though. He hardly ever talked, and Natalie had to use every trick in the book to get him to participate. Natalie stayed focused during her sessions with Sam because, well, she was a professional, but she got little satisfaction out of it. Sam remained obstinate and grumpy no matter what Natalie did.

During one of their conferences, Natalie challenged Sam about an opinion he had expressed in a recent essay. She asked Sam how he had formulated this particular opinion, and why he had chosen to write about it. After Natalie asked her question, Sam slammed some papers onto the table and shouted, "It's none of your business! Can't you just leave me alone?!" Sam then stood up, gathered his things, and walked out of the classroom.

Natalie sat there for a few moments. She knew Sam was difficult but not this difficult. After she composed herself, she went in search of him and discovered him by his locker. When she approached him, Sam again told her to leave him alone.

"What's going on, Sam?" Natalie said. "We need to talk. I'm sorry if I said something to offend you, but your behavior is unacceptable. Let's go back to the classroom and finish our session and later we can discuss what happened."

"No!" shouted Sam, and he ran down the hallway, leaving Natalie stunned and angry. Natalie's next conversation was with Don, the assistant principal, who agreed that Sam needed to face some consequences for his behavior. Don said he would summon Sam to his office and keep Natalie posted.

Natalie was surprised to see Sam in class the next day. He was his same unpleasant self, but Natalie felt encouraged that he showed up at all. Later that day, Don reported to Natalie that he'd given Sam a detention for his behavior, so Natalie decided to wait until his next conference before saying anything to him.

When Sam showed up for the conference, he acted as though nothing had happened. Natalie took her cue from him and stayed focused on their work. As long as he showed up, Natalie took this as a good sign. During this conference, however, Sam was a little more forthcoming and cooperative when Natalie tried to engage him about his work. It was still difficult from Natalie's perspective but it was something.

Throughout the remainder of the year, Natalie and Sam continued to meet during their conference time. There were no more outbursts on Sam's part, but he didn't improve much as a student, either. Natalie stayed as focused and positive as possible, and she treated Sam like she treated her other students.

The year came and went. Sam graduated. Natalie wasn't even sure what his plans for college were. He didn't say goodbye.

About a year later, Natalie received an email from Sam. He told her what he was doing, that he liked school (she was sort of surprised to learn he had even gone to college), and how much he appreciated all she'd done for him. Sam told Natalie that he had been going through a very tough time during his senior year. He'd hated himself and life, and he hated it when anyone paid attention to him, as Natalie had. He apologized for his behavior. He hadn't meant to be so rude, he said, but sometimes he just got upset and didn't know how to deal with it.

At the end of the note, Sam told Natalie that having her as his English teacher was one of the high points of his senior year. He admitted that she had irritated him at the time, but after he graduated, he realized Natalie was the one person who really cared about him at school; she was the one person who didn't give up on him. Even though he didn't appreciate it then, Sam said he was grateful Natalie didn't hold his behavior against him, and that she cared enough to stay engaged with him despite his attempts to push her away.

We really do matter.

Appendix

RELAXATION EXERCISES

Practicing relaxation and stress reduction exercises throughout the school day is an excellent form of self-care. The goal of any relaxation protocol is to calm the heart rate, quiet the mind, and refresh the spirit. This can be done in countless ways; what's important is that we find a way that works for us and then work our method into our daily schedules.

The following are two kinds of relaxation exercises. The first is called a "mini," and it can be done in just a minute or two at any point throughout the day. The second group of exercises are longer and can be used with students. I suggest we practice our own method of relaxation before introducing these exercises to students. Our success in passing this information along to students is greatly enhanced when we've mastered some of these methods first.

The following relaxation exercises are reprinted with permission of the Benson-Henry Institute of Mind Body Medicine, Massachusetts General Hospital.° Whereas these relaxation protocols can be used as standalone exercises, I urge interested readers to refer to *The Relaxation Response*, by Dr. Herbert Benson, for a more comprehensive understanding of stress and mind-body relaxation.

MINI RELAXATION EXERCISES (1–2 MINUTES)

Mini relaxation exercises, or "minis," are focused techniques, which help reduce anxiety and tension immediately.

Ways to do a "mini":

1. Count very slowly to yourself from ten down to zero, one number for each breath. Thus, with the first complete inhalation and exhalation, you say *ten* to yourself; with the next, *nine*, and so on. If you start feeling light-headed or dizzy, slow down the counting. When you get to zero, see how you are feeling. If you are feeling better, great! If not, try doing it again.
2. As you inhale, say to yourself *one, two, three, four*, as you exhale, say to yourself *four, three, two, one*. Do this several times.
3. After each inhalation, pause for a few seconds; after you exhale, pause again for a few seconds. Do this for several breaths.

Good times to do a "mini":

- while stuck in traffic
- when put on hold during an important phone call
- while waiting in your doctor's waiting room
- when someone says something that bothers you
- at all red lights
- when waiting for a phone call
- in the dentist's chair
- when you feel overwhelmed by what you need to accomplish
- while standing in line
- when in pain

Remember, the only time minis don't work is when you forget to do them!

LONGER RELAXATION EXERCISES (ABOUT 12 MINUTES)

These longer exercises should be read aloud to students, other adults, or into a tape recorder for your own use. I recommend introducing such exercises to students as part of a unit on health or stress reduction, or as part of the physical education or athletics curriculum. Students generally need a context for understanding this kind of thing, or at least high school students do (in my experience, younger students are receptive even without a lot of context). Older students are more amenable once they grasp the benefits of relaxation. Of course, any teacher can use these exercises in any setting but students often need to be prepped.

As in all aspects of learning, repetition is key, so I suggest we set aside regular times to do this with our students. They won't gain much benefit if they practice this sporadically, although even a little relaxation is better than nothing. Once students are established in the longer protocols, then they are ready for "minis." We need to teach our bodies and minds how to relax before we can effectively use these shorter, albeit very effective exercises throughout the day.

Exercise 1

Note: If you read this out loud, pause often and keep a steady tone without becoming monotone. Be aware that you might pick up your pace as you near the end of the exercise.

Before we begin this relaxation, think of a place where you feel comfortable, relaxed, safe, and at ease. It can be inside or outdoors, maybe a room in your home or a mansion, or on a beach or a mountain. This can be a place you've visited, or seen a picture of, or it can be a place you invent right now. [*Pause.*] Whatever place you think of, where it's comfortable for you, is fine.

If you choose, you can put your head down on your desk, and gently close your eyes. If you prefer, you might look down at your hands in your lap or at a spot on the floor. If you need to open your eyes, you can open them at any time. This is a rest, a short vacation, for your body and your mind. If you don't want to participate, that's fine, but please sit quietly and don't disturb those who are participating.

Now that you have your relaxing place in your mind, settle in, and you'll spend the next few minutes listening to the sound of my voice. If other noises interfere, you can notice them, and then just let them go, and return to the sound of my voice.

Now, become aware of your breath, breathing in slow, easy breaths. Feel how your breath moves down into your belly. Breathe in a feeling of quiet and calm. Let your breath help release any tension or stress. Breathe in peace; breathe out tension and anxiety. Let the relaxation get deeper, easier; don't force your breath. Just feel the rhythm of your breathing. [*Pause.*] As you let go of any negative thoughts, putting them aside for now, feel how your body relaxes.

And now, think of relaxing, warm light, like the sun, passing down over you, down from the top of your head. Down from your head, warming and relaxing your eyes, and your cheeks, down to your jaw. The warm light is moving down your neck, warming and releasing any tension in your neck, warming down your shoulders, releasing tension in your shoulders, as you continue to breathe in a feeling of calm and peace, and breathe out tension.

The warmth relaxes down your shoulders, moving down your arms, allowing tension to release off your fingertips.

[*Slowly.*] The warm light moves down your upper back, to your lower back, down your legs, to your toes, where tension is released and washed away to the floor, leaving you relaxed and calm.

Now, as you continue to breathe gently and calmly, in easy, comfortable breaths, become aware again, of being in your special place. [*Pause.*] Notice what you see around you, [*pause*] if there are any sounds you hear, or any familiar smells. If you're indoors, you might notice any details about the space you're in; the way the light falls. Outside, you might notice if there's a breeze, or the temperature of the air around you.

Whatever you need is here, because you've created this place. If you want to sit down and rest, there might be a soft chair if you're inside, or a hammock if you're outdoors. Whatever is most comfortable for you. [*Pause.*] Whatever you see, or hear, or touch or smell is fine, as you relax, and allow yourself to rest in the comfort of this place. [*Pause.*] As you think of yourself in this place, appreciate the comfort here, how safe it is, breathing in a sense of calm and peace, breathing out tension. And know that you can return, that you can go to this place, your place, whenever you need to relax, or feel comfortable and quiet. Whenever you need a rest from the day, you can see yourself in this place, and give yourself a moment of quiet and relaxation.

Now, gently become aware of your breath, and notice how rested your body feels. [*Pause.*] Become aware of your feet on the floor, of sitting. Think of this room you're sitting in before opening your eyes. Before opening your eyes, notice any sounds in the room around you.

You might stretch your fingers, hands, and feet. Now, slowly open your eyes, and return to the room, feeling relaxed and contented. Feeling refreshed and alert, with a sense of accomplishment in what you have just experienced.

Exercise 2: Breath Focus and Word/Phrase Focus Relaxation Response

Note: You may choose to use music as a background with this exercise. This relaxation takes approximately twelve minutes, through it can be longer or shorter depending upon how long you pause between sections. The indicated pause times are suggestions only.

This is a breath-focused exercise. Now, please get comfortable and if it feels right for you, close your eyes. If you are not comfortable closing your eyes, look down at your hands or at your desktop.

[Pause for five seconds.]

With your eyes closed, turn your attention to your breathing. Relaxed breathing is deep and slow. Bring your attention to the way you breathe.

[Pause for five seconds.]

When we are breathing in a relaxed way, our stomach rises with each breath in, and falls slightly with each breath out. So, focus for a moment on your breathing.

[Pause for ten seconds.]

Now, notice the cool air entering your nostrils. See if you can follow the breath down into your lungs.

[Pause for ten seconds.]

Now, notice the warm air as it leaves your body.

[Pause for ten seconds.]

Become aware of how the muscles in your body are affected by your breath. Notice the muscles across your back moving with each breath.

[Pause for ten seconds.]

Notice the muscles along your arms and through your stomach. Try to become aware of all the muscle groups affected by your breathing.

[Pause for ten seconds.]

Now imagine that you are breathing in peace with each breath.

[Pause for five seconds.]

Imagine that you are breathing out tension and anxiety.

[*Pause for five seconds.*]

Breathe in peace. Breathe out tension and anxiety.

[*Pause for twenty seconds.*]

If thoughts intrude on your mind, just notice, and then let them go. Bring your mind back to your breathing.

[*Pause for ten seconds.*]

Another way to keep your mind focused is by using a word or phrase, and repeating that word or phrase in rhythm with your breathing. You can choose a word that gives you a feeling of relaxation. Some people choose a word like *peace*, or *calm*, or maybe *ocean*, which brings an image of the beauty of the ocean. Some people use a phrase such as "I am calm and quiet" or "I am strong and stable." Others like to use the name of a person who helps them feel relaxed, or even a piece of a prayer if they are religious. Choose whatever feels right for you.

[*Pause for ten seconds.*]

Now that you have your word or phrase or name, simply use it as a focus, repeating it in rhythm with your breathing. Take your time.

[*Pause for twenty seconds.*]If you lose your focus, just bring your mind back to your focus word or phrase or name.

[*Pause for twenty seconds. As this type of focused relaxation becomes more familiar for your students, you can increase the time up to several minutes.*]

You can use your breath focus and your word focus techniques at any time during the day when you want to relax.

[*Pause for ten seconds.*]

Now I'm going to count from five to one. When I reach one, you'll bring your attention back to the room, refreshed and alert. At five, you feel how relaxed you've become. At four, you begin to bring your awareness to your body, and how it feels to be sitting in your chair. At three, you become aware of the sounds around you, you can feel the energy returning to your body, but you will carry the peacefulness of this moment with you through your day. At two, you feel the energy returning to your body, and at one, *eyes open, wide awake.*

NOTE

°For further information, please contact Marilyn Wilcher, senior director (617-643-6035, mwilcher@partners.org) or Rana Chudnofsky (617-643-6068, rchudnofsky@partners.org).

BIBLIOGRAPHY AND RESOURCES

Baird, A. A., & Fuglesang, J. (2004). The Emergence of Consequential Thought: Evidence from Neuroscience. *Philosophical Transactions of the Royal Society, vol. 359*, 1797–1804.

Benson, H., & Klipper, M. (2000). *The Relaxation Response*. New York: Harper Paperbacks.

Blos, P. (1967). The Second Individuation Process of Adolescence. *Psychoanalytic Study of the Child*, 162–86.

Conkle, A. (2007). Decisions, Decisions [electronic version]. *Observer*, Association for Psychological Science, 20, number 7.

Freud, S., & Strachey, J. (1962). *The Ego and the Id (The Standard Edition of the Complete Psychological Works of Sigmund Freud)*. New York: W. W. Norton.

Merriam-Webster. (2008). Merriam-Webster Online Dictionary.

Society of Neuroscience. (2007). The Adolescent Brain [electronic version].*Society of Neuroscience*.

Strauch, B. (2004). *The Primal Teen: What the New Discoveries about the Teenage Brain Tell Us about Our Kids*. New York: Doubleday.

U.S. Department of Education, Office of the Under Secretary. (2004). *Educator Sexual Misconduct: A Synthesis of Existing Literature*, Washington, D.C.

RESOURCES

1. Relaxation and Stress Reduction in Schools:

   Benson-Henry Institute for Mind Body Medicine. www.mbmi.org

2. Workshop on Counseling for Independent School Educators:

   Stanley H. King Counseling Institute for Independent Secondary Schools. www.shkingcounseling.org

3. Annual Conference on the Brain and Learning:

   Learning and the Brain, National Conference on Learning and the Brain for Parents, Teachers, Administrators, Clinicians and Adult Trainers. www.edupr.com

4. Books on Adolescent Development for Educators:

   Daniels, D., & Meece, J. (2007). *Child and Adolescent Development for Educators, 3rd Edition*. New York: McGraw-Hill.
   Defrates-Densch, N. (2007). *Cases in Child and Adolescent Development for Teachers*. New York: McGraw-Hill.
   McCormick, C., & Pressley, M. (2006). *Child and Adolescent Development for Educators*. New York: Guilford Press.
   Nakkula, M., & Toshalis, E. (2006). *Understanding Youth*. Cambridge, MA: Harvard Education Press.

ABOUT THE AUTHOR

Susan Eva Porter began her teaching career at Phillips Exeter Academy, where she started the academy's health education program. She has since worked at public and private day schools on the East and West Coasts. She received her bachelor's degree from Brown University and has graduate degrees in education, clinical social work, and clinical psychology. Susan served on the adjunct faculty at the Smith College School for Social Work, and is currently in private practice as an educational and clinical consultant to schools and individuals in San Francisco.